THE HAZARDOUS EARTH

ASTEROIDS AND METEORITES

Catastrophic Collisions with Earth

Timothy Kusky, Ph.D.

Facts On File
An imprint of Infobase Publishing

To the pioneers from and affiliated with NASA who gave their lives
in the exploration of the solar system.

This includes test pilots Theodore Freeman, Elliott See, Charles Bassett, Clifton Williams,
Michael Adams, Robert Lawrence, and M. L. Sonny Carter; the Apollo 1 *astronauts Gus Grissom,*
Ed White, and Roger Chaffee; the crew of space shuttle Challenger, *including Francis Scobee,*
Michael Smith, Ronald McNair, Gregory Jarvis, Judith Resnik, Ellison Onizuka, and Christa McAuliffe;
the crew of space shuttle Columbia, *including Rick D. Husband, William C. McCool,*
Michael P. Anderson, David M. Brown, Kalpana Chawla, Laurel Clark, and Ilan Ramon.

■ ■ ■

ASTEROIDS AND METEORITES: Catastrophic Collisions with Earth

Copyright © 2009 by Timothy Kusky, Ph.D.

Facts On File, Inc.
An imprint of Infobase Publishing
132 West 31st Street
New York NY 10001

Library of Congress Cataloging-in-Publication Data
Kusky, Timothy M.
  Asteroids and meteorites : catastrophic collisions with Earth / Timothy Kusky.
      p. cm.— (The hazardous Earth)
  Includes bibliographical references and index.
  ISBN-13: 978-0-8160-6469-4
  ISBN-10: 0-8160-6469-5
  1. Asteroids—Collisions with Earth. 2. Meteorites. 3. Catastrophes (Geology) I. Title.
  QB651.K87 2009
  551.3'97—dc22   2008007897

Facts On File books are available at special discounts when purchased in bulk
quantities for businesses, associations, institutions, or sales promotions. Please call our Special Sales Department in New York at (212) 967-8800 or (800) 322-8755.

You can find Facts On File on the World Wide Web at http://www.factsonfile.com

Text design by Erika K. Arroyo
Illustrations by Richard Garratt
Photo research by Suzanne M. Tibor

Printed in the United States of America

VB FOF 10 9 8 7 6 5 4 3 2 1

This book is printed on acid-free paper and contains 30 percent postconsumer recycled contents.

Contents

Preface

Natural geologic hazards arise from the interaction between humans and the Earth's natural processes. Recent natural disasters such as the 2004 Indian Ocean tsunami that killed more than a quarter million people and earthquakes in Iran, Turkey, and Japan have shown how the motion of the Earth's tectonic plates can suddenly make apparently safe environments dangerous or even deadly. The slow sinking of the land surface along many seashores has made many of the world's coastal regions prone to damage by ocean storms, as shown disastrously by Hurricane Katrina in 2005. Other natural Earth hazards arise gradually, such as the migration of poisonous radon gas into people's homes. Knowledge of Earth's natural hazards can lead one to live a safer life, providing guidance on where to build homes, where to travel, and what to do during natural hazard emergencies.

The eight-volume The Hazardous Earth set is intended to provide middle- and high-school students and college students with a readable yet comprehensive account of natural geologic hazards—the geologic processes that create conditions hazardous to humans—and what can be done to minimize their effects. Titles in the set present clear descriptions of plate tectonics and associated hazards, including earthquakes, volcanic eruptions, landslides, and soil and mineral hazards, as well as hazards resulting from the interaction of the ocean, atmosphere, and land, such as tsunamis, hurricanes, floods, and drought. After providing the reader with an in-depth knowledge of naturally hazardous processes, each volume gives vivid accounts of historic disasters and events that have shaped human history and serve as reminders for future generations.

One volume covers the basic principles of plate tectonics and earthquake hazards, and another volume covers hazards associated with volcanoes. A third volume is about tsunamis and related wave phenomena, and another volume covers landslides, soil, and mineral hazards, and includes discussions of mass wasting processes, soils, and the dangers of the natural concentration of hazardous elements such as radon. A fifth volume covers hazards resulting from climate change and drought, and how they affect human populations. That volume also discusses glacial environments and landforms, shifting climates, and desertification—all related to the planet's oscillations from ice ages to hothouses. Greater understanding is achieved by discussing environments on Earth that resemble icehouse (glaciers) and hothouse (desert) conditions. A sixth volume, entitled *The Coast,* includes discussion of hazards associated with hurricanes, coastal subsidence, and the impact of building along coastlines. A seventh volume, *Floods,* discusses river flooding and flood disasters, as well as many of the contemporary issues associated with the world's diminishing freshwater supply in the face of a growing population. This book also includes a chapter on sinkholes and phenomena related to water overuse. An eighth volume, *Asteroids and Meteorites,* presents information on impacts that have affected the Earth, their effects, and the chances that another impact may occur soon on Earth.

The Hazardous Earth set is intended overall to be a reference book set for middle school, high school, and undergraduate college students, teachers and professors, scientists, librarians, journalists, and anyone who may be looking for information about Earth processes that may be hazardous to humans. The set is well illustrated with photographs and other illustrations, including line art, graphs, and tables. Each volume stands alone and can also be used in sequence with other volumes of the set in a natural hazards or disasters curriculum.

Acknowledgments

Many people have helped me with different aspects of preparing this volume. I would especially like to thank Carolyn, my wife, and my children, Shoshana and Daniel, for their patience during the long hours spent at my desk preparing this book. Without their understanding this work would not have been possible. Frank Darmstadt, executive editor, reviewed and edited all text and figures, providing guidance and consistency throughout. The excellent photo research provided by Suzie Tibor is appreciated and she is responsible for locating many of the excellent photographs in this volume. Many sections of the work draw from my own experiences doing scientific research in different parts of the world, and it is not possible to thank the hundreds of colleagues whose collaborations and work I have related in this book. Their contributions to the science that allowed the writing of this volume are greatly appreciated. I extend special thanks to two individuals who sparked my interest in meteoritics and impacts, Karl Ritchie, and John Delano. I have tried to reference the most relevant works, or in some cases more recent sources that have more extensive reference lists. Any omissions are unintentional.

Introduction

*A*steroids and comets are space objects that orbit the Sun. When these objects enter the Earth's atmosphere they may make a streak of light known as a *meteor,* and if they are not burned up in the atmosphere the remaining rocky or metallic body is known as a *meteorite.* By definition, asteroids are a class of minor *planets* that have a diameter less than 620 miles (1,000 km), whereas planets are roughly spherical objects that orbit the Sun and have a diameter greater than 620 miles (1,000 km). *Comets* are partly icy bodies that may have rocky cores, and typically orbit the Sun in highly elliptical paths. Most streaks of light known as meteors are produced by microscopic or dust-sized particles entering the atmosphere. Larger objects falling to Earth from space make a larger streak of light known as a *fireball* as they burn up on entry through the atmosphere.

Earth formed through the *accretion* of many asteroids about 4.5 billion years ago. As the solar system was condensing from a spinning disk of gas and dust particles, these particles began to collide, sometimes sticking to other particles. Gradually the particles became bigger and bigger until they were large rocky and metallic asteroids, which collided with each other until some became so large that they began collecting other asteroids through their gravitational attraction. These *proto-planets* swept their orbits clear of other asteroids, and gradually grew larger in the process. Many of the proto-planets grew large enough to start to melt internally, and produce layered planetary bodies with dense cores, and lighter crusts. At this late stage, many proto-planets, including the

Artist's rendition of a massive impact hitting Earth—note the vaporization of the atmosphere and the shock waves spreading out from the point of impact *(David A. Hardy/ Photo Researchers)*

Earth, experienced collisions with other large proto-planets, causing catastrophic melting and fragmentation of the earliest planetary crusts. As this late-stage accretion period ended, the Earth went through a period called the late bombardment, when many smaller meteorites were still falling to Earth, causing local disruption of the crust. Since then the number of meteorites that hit the Earth has been gradually decreasing, but in the rare events when medium or large objects from space hit the Earth, the results can be devastating.

Meteorites are rocky objects from space that strike the Earth. When meteorites pass through Earth's atmosphere, they get heated and their surfaces become ionized, causing them to glow brightly, forming a streak moving across the atmosphere known as a shooting star or fireball. If the meteorite is large enough it may not burn up in the atmosphere and will then strike the Earth. Small meteorites may just crash on the surface, but the rare, large object can excavate a large *impact crater,* or do worse damage. At certain times of the year the Earth passes through parts of the solar system that are rich in meteorites, and the night skies become filled with shooting stars and fireballs, sometimes as frequently as several per minute. These times of high-frequency meteorite encounters are known as meteor showers, and include the Perseid showers that appear around August 11, and the Leonid showers that appear about November 14.

It is now recognized that an impact with a space object, probably a meteorite, caused the extinction of the dinosaurs and 65 percent of all the other species on the planet at the end of the Cretaceous Period 66 millions years ago. The meteor impact crater is apparently preserved at Chicxulub on Mexico's Yucatán Peninsula, and the impact occurred at a time when the world's biosphere was already stressed, probably by massive amounts of volcanism, global atmospheric change, and sea-level fall. The volcanic fields that were being laid down for a few million years before the *mass extinction* and death of the dinosaurs are preserved as vast lava plains in western India known as the Deccan traps. Impacts and massive volcanism can both dramatically change the global climate on scales that far exceed the changes witnessed in the past few thousands of years, or in the past hundred years as a result of human activities such as the burning of fossil fuels. These changes have dramatic influences on evolution and extinction of species and current ideas suggest that impacts and volcanism have been responsible for most of the great extinctions of geological time.

Impacts cause earthquakes of unimaginable magnitude, thousands of times stronger than any ever observed on Earth by humans. If a large meteorite lands in the ocean, it can form giant *tsunamis* hundreds if not thousands of feet (m) tall that sweep across ocean basins in minutes, and run up hundreds of miles (km) onto the continents. Impacts kick up tremendous amounts of dust and hot flaming gases that scorch the atmosphere and fill it with sun-blocking dust clouds for years. Global fires burn most organic matter in a global fireball, and these fires are followed by a period of dark deep freeze, caused by the atmospheric dust blocking out warming sunlight. This may be followed rapidly by a warm period after the dust settles, caused by the extra carbon dioxide released in the atmosphere by the impact. These severe and rapid changes in atmospheric and oceanic temperature and chemistry kill off many of the remaining life-forms in the oceans.

This book examines the character of asteroids, comets, and meteorites, and the consequences of the impact of these extraterrestrial bodies from elsewhere in the solar system with the Earth. The first chapter reviews the origin of the solar system, including the formation and relationships between the Sun, planets, asteroids, and comets. The role of impacts of asteroids with each other in forming the early Earth is discussed. The second chapter looks at the origin of meteorites, asteroids, and comets, showing where they are located in the solar system, and discussing different models for their origin. The third chapter describes many of the craters on Earth that have formed as a result of meteorites or asteroids crashing into the planet, with such force that they excavate huge holes and wreak widespread destruction on the landscape. It also examines the physical processes that occur during the impact of these objects with the Earth, including small objects that vaporize in the atmosphere, to the largest impacts that may vaporize large portions of the global oceans when they hit. Several specific cases of impacts are presented, and the consequences for the biosphere discussed. Chapter 4 presents a historical perspective on the relationships between impacts and life on Earth, examining impacts that have been suggested to have caused mass extinctions of fauna and flora on global scales, including the famous extinction of the dinosa urs. Specific examples of the impacts associated with these events are discussed, and then the role of impacts and noncatastrophic processes for the history and future of life on Earth are examined. The fifth chapter looks at the specific hazards associated with large and small impacts, including earthquakes, shock waves, giant tsunamis, and global firestorms, and blocking of the sun resulting in global winter. This is followed by a discussion of the different ways that nations of the world may be able to act to monitor the paths of space objects, and know better how and when to prepare for the next major impact on Earth.

1

Origin of Planets, Asteroids, and Comets

Collisions of asteroids with each other in the early history of the solar system led to the formation of planets, but left many asteroids and other debris scattered at different places in the solar system. After the initial periods of accretion of the planets the bombardment of the planets by asteroids decreased, but some bodies still fell to the planet as meteorites. Most were small and burned up before they hit the surface, but others have inflicted tremendous disruption to the planet. However, collisions of comets with Earth is largely responsible for bringing the lighter volatile elements, including those that comprise the planet's air and oceans, to Earth. It is also probable that asteroids or comets brought primitive organic molecules or even life to the planet.

Origin of the Universe

Cosmologists, scientists who study the origin and evolution of the universe, estimate that the universe is 10 to 20 billion years old, and consists of a huge number of stars grouped in galaxies, clusters of galaxies, and superclusters of galaxies, surrounded by vast distances of open space. The universe is thought to be expanding because measurements show that the most distant galaxies, quasars, and most other objects in the universe are moving away from each other and from the center of the universe. The *big bang theory* states that the expanding universe originated 10 to 20 billion years ago in a single explosive event in which the entire universe suddenly exploded out of nothing, reaching a pea-sized supercondensed state with a temperature of 10 billion million million degrees Celsius in one million-million-million-million-million-millionth (10^{-36}) of a second after the big bang. Some of the fundamental parts of the expanding universe models come from Albert Einstein (1879–1955), who in 1915 proposed the General Theory of Relativity relating how matter and energy warp space-time to produce gravity. When Einstein applied his theory to the universe in 1917, he discovered that gravity would cause the universe to be unstable and collapse, so he proposed adding a cosmological constant as a "fudge factor" to his equations. The cosmological constant added a repulsive force to the General Theory, and this force counterbalanced gravity enabling the universe to continue expanding in his equations. Willem de Sitter (1872–1934) further applied Einstein's General Theory of Relativity to predict that the universe is expanding. In 1927, Georges Lemaître (1894–1966) proposed that the universe originated in a giant explosion of a primeval atom, an event that is now called the "big bang." In 1929, Edwin Hubble (1889–1953) measured the movement of distant galaxies and discovered that galaxies are moving away from each other, expanding the universe as if the universe is being propelled from a big bang. This idea of expansion from an explosion negated the need for Einstein's cosmological constant, which he retracted, referring to it as his biggest blunder. This retraction, however, would later come back to haunt cosmologists.

Also in the 1920s, George Gamow (1904–68) worked with a group of scientists and suggested that elements heavier than hydrogen, specifically helium and lithium, could be produced in thermonuclear reactions during the big bang. Later, in 1957, Fred Hoyle (1915–2001), William Fowler (1911–95), and Geoff and Margaret Burbidge (1925– , 1919–) showed how hydrogen and helium could be processed in stars to produce heavier elements such as carbon, oxygen, and iron, necessary for life.

The *inflationary theory* is a modification of the big bang theory, and suggests that the universe underwent a period of rapid expansion immediately after the big bang. Alan Guth (1947–) proposed this theory in 1980, and it attempts to explain the present distribution of galaxies, as well as the 3°K cosmic background radiation discovered by Arno Penzias (1933–) and Robert Wilson (1936–) in 1965. This uniformly distributed radiation is thought to be a relict left over from the initial explosion of the big bang. For many years after the discovery of the cosmic background radiation, astronomers searched for answers to the amount of mass in the universe and to determine how fast the universe was expanding, and how much the gravitational attraction of bodies in the universe was causing the expansion to slow. A relatively high density of matter in the universe would cause it to eventually decelerate and collapse back upon itself, forming a "Big Crunch," and perhaps a new big bang. Cosmologists called this the closed universe model. A low-density universe would expand forever, forming what cosmologists called an open universe. In between these end member models was a "flat" universe that would expand ever more slowly until it froze in place.

In the *standard model* for the universe, the big bang occurred 14 billion years ago and marked the beginning of the universe. The cause and reasons for the big bang are not part of the theory, but left for the fields of religion and philosophy. Dr. William Percival of the University of Edinburgh leads a group of standard model cosmologists, and they calculate that the big bang occurred 13.89 billion years ago, plus or minus half a billion years. Most of the matter of the universe is proposed to reside in huge invisible clouds of *dark matter,* thought to contain elementary particles left over from the big bang. Galaxies and stars reside in these huge clouds of matter, and comprise a mere 4.8 percent of the matter in the universe. The dark matter forms 22.7 percent of the universe, leaving another 72.5 percent of the universe as nonmatter. At the time of the proposal of the standard model, this ambiguous dark matter had yet to be conclusively detected or identified. In 2002, the first-ever atoms of antimatter were captured and analyzed by scientific teams from CERN, the European Laboratory for Particle Physics.

Detailed observations of the *cosmic background radiation* by spaceborne platforms such as NASA's *COBE (Cosmic Background Explorer)* that in 1992 revealed faint variations and structure in the background radiation, consistent with an inflationary expanding universe. Blotches and patterns in the background radiation reveal areas that may have been the seeds or spawning grounds for the origin of galaxies and clusters. Detailed measurements of this background radiation have revealed that the universe is best thought of as flat. However, the lack of sufficient observable matter to have a flat universe requires the existence of some invisible dark matter. These observations were further expanded in 2002, when teams working with the *DASI (Degree Angular Scale Interferometer)* experiment reported directional differences (called polarizations) in the cosmic microwave background radiation dating from 450,000 years after the big bang. The astronomers were able to relate these directional differences to forces that led to the formation of galaxies and the overall structure of the universe today. These density differences are quantum effects that effectively seeded the early universe with protogalaxies during the early inflation period, and their observation provides strong support for the standard model for the universe.

Recent measurements have shown that the rate of expansion of the universe seems to be increasing, which has led cosmologists to propose the presence of a dark energy that is presently largely unknown. This dark energy is thought to comprise the remaining 72.5 percent of the universe, and it is analogous to a repulsive force or antimatter. Recognition in 1998 that the universe is expanding at ever increasing rates has toppled questions about open versus closed universe models, and has drastically changed perceptions of the fate of the universe. Amazingly, the rate of acceleration of expansion is remarkably consistent with Einstein's abandoned cosmological constant. The expansion seems to be accelerating so fast that eventually, the galaxies will be moving apart so fast, they will not be able to see each other and the universe will become dark. Other cosmologists argue that so little is known of dark matter and dark energy that it is difficult to predict how it will act in the future, and the fate of the universe is not determinable from our present observations.

Alan Guth and coworkers have recently proposed modifications of the inflationary universe model. They propose that the initial inflation of the universe, in its first few microseconds, can happen over and over again, forming an endless chain of universes, called multiverses by Dr. Martin Rees (1942–   ) of Cambridge University. With these ideas, our 14 billion-year-old universe may be just one of many, with big bangs causing inflations of the perhaps infinite other universes. According to the theories of particle physics it takes only about one ounce of primordial starting material to inflate to a universe like our own. The process of growing chains of bubble-like universes through multiple big bangs and inflationary events has been termed eternal inflation by Dr. Andrei Linde (1948–   ) of Stanford University.

Cosmologists, astronomers, and physicists are searching for a grand unifying theory that is able to link Einstein's General Relativity with quantum mechanics, and new observations of our universe. One attempt at a grand unifying theory is the string theory, in which elementary particles are thought to be analogous to notes being played on strings vibrating in 10- or 11-dimensional space. A newer theory emerging is called M-theory, or Matrix theory, in which various dimensional membranes including universes can interact and collide, setting off big bangs and expansions that could continue or alternate indefinitely.

Cosmology and the fate of theories like the big bang are undergoing rapid and fundamental changes in understanding, induced by new technologies, computing abilities, philosophy, and from the asking of new questions about creation of the universe. Although it is tempting to think of current theories as complete, perhaps with a few unanswered questions, history tells us that much can change with a few new observations, questions, or understanding.

The Solar System

The Solar System represents the remnants of a *solar nebula* that formed in one of the spiral arms of the Milky Way galaxy. After the condensation of the nebula, the solar system consisted of eight major planets, the moons of these planets, and many smaller bodies in interplanetary space. From the Sun outward, these planetary bodies include Mercury, Venus, Earth, Mars, the asteroids, Jupiter, Saturn, Uranus, and Neptune. Until 2007 Pluto was regarded as a planet, but as discussed in the sidebar on page 8, in 2006 a team of astronomers voted that Pluto did not meet the criteria of being a planet, in that its orbit was too erratic, its size too small, and demoted Pluto to the status equivalent of a captured asteroid. Most asteroids are concentrated in a broad band called the asteroid belt located between the orbits of Mars and Jupiter. Although none of the asteroids are larger than Earth's moon, they are considered by many to be "minor planets," since they are orbiting the Sun.

The asteroids are small rocky and metallic bodies most of which orbit in the asteroid belt located between Mars and Jupiter. Other asteroids have different erratic orbits, and others are located in different belts further from the Sun. Comets include icy bodies and rocky bodies, and are thought by many astronomers to be material that is left over from the formation of the Solar System, and that was not incorporated into any planetary bodies. Thus, comets may have clues about the early composition of the solar nebula.

The planets and asteroids orbit the Sun counterclockwise when viewed from above Earth's North Pole, and most have roughly circular orbits that are confined to a relatively flat plane called the *ecliptic plane*. The spacing between the different orbits increases with increasing distance from the Sun. The inner four planets have densities and properties that are roughly similar to Earth, and are referred to as the terrestrial planets, and are generally rocky in character. In contrast the

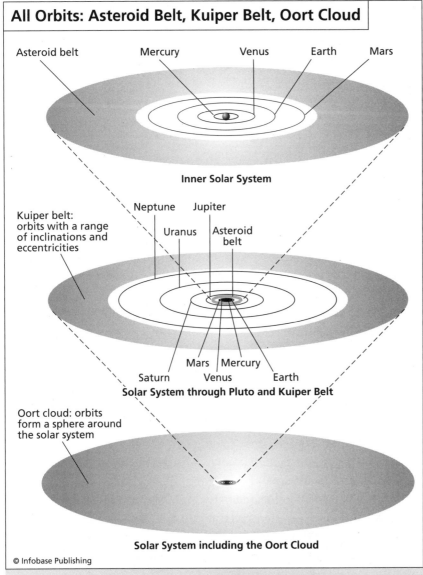

All Orbits: Asteroid Belt, Kuiper Belt, Oort Cloud

Asteroid belt   Mercury   Venus   Earth   Mars

Inner Solar System

Kuiper belt:
orbits with a range
of inclinations and
eccentricities

Neptune   Jupiter

Uranus   Asteroid
belt

Mars   Mercury

Saturn   Venus   Earth

Solar System through Pluto and Kuiper Belt

Oort cloud: orbits
form a sphere around
the solar system

Solar System including the Oort Cloud

© Infobase Publishing

Diagram showing the relative arrangement of major bodies of the solar system, including the planets, main asteroid belt, Kuiper Belt, and Oort Cloud

outer planets (Jupiter, Saturn, Uranus, and Neptune) have much lower densities and are mostly gaseous or liquid in form, and are generally known as the Jovian planets. The Jovian planets are much more massive than the terrestrial planets, rotate more rapidly, have stronger magnetic fields than the terrestrial planets, and have systems of rings that circle the planets.

Properties of Objects in Solar System

OBJECT	ORBITAL DISTANCE (AU)	MASS (EARTHS)	DIAMETER (EARTHS)	ROTATIONAL PERIOD (YEARS) (- MEANS RETROGRADE)	ORBITAL PERIOD (YEARS)	DENSITY (EARTHS)	SURFACE GRAVITY (EARTHS)	MOONS
Sun	0.0	332,000	109.2	25.8	...	1.42	28	...
Mercury	0.39	0.06	0.38	59	0.24	0.98	0.38	0
Venus	0.72	0.81	0.95	-243	0.62	0.95	0.90	0
Earth	1.0	1.00	1.00	1.00	1.0	1.00	1.00	1
Mars	1.5	0.11	0.53	1.03	1.9	0.71	0.38	2
Ceres asteroid	2.8	0.0002	0.07	0.38	4.7	0.38	0.03	0
Jupiter	5.2	317.8	11.2	0.42	11.9	0.24	2.34	63
Saturn	9.5	95.2	9.5	0.44	29.5	0.12	1.16	60
Uranus	19.2	14.5	4.0	-0.69	83.7	0.23	1.15	27
Neptune	30.1	17.2	3.9	0.72	163.7	0.30	1.19	13
Pluto (dwarf planet)	39.5	0.002	0.18	-6.40	248.0	0.37	0.04	3
Eris (dwarf planet discovered June 2007)	67.7	0.002	0.18	~8	557	?	?	1

IS PLUTO A PLANET?

The solar system has long been considered to have nine planets, including Mercury, Venus, Earth, Mars, Jupiter, Saturn, Uranus, Neptune, and Pluto. Pluto has been thought to be the most distant planet, and a relatively small body at roughly one fifth the mass of Earth's moon, or 0.66 percent of Earth's volume. Pluto is considerably smaller than many Moons in the solar system, including Ganymede, Titan, Callisto, Io, Earth's Moon, Europa, and Triton. In 2006 the International Astronomical Union met, and decided that Pluto does not meet the formal criteria of being a planet, and demoted the status of the object to that of a *"dwarf planet."* What happened?

Pluto has a colorful history of discovery. In the early to mid 1800s scientists noticed that the orbit of Uranus showed some unusual perturbations, and hypothesized that these were due to the gravitational attraction of a more distant planet, and were able to predict where a new planet, Neptune should be. French mathematician Urbain Le Verrier (1811–77) performed these calculations, and then sent his calculation of where this planet should be to German astronomer Johann Gottfried Galle (1812–1910) on September 23, 1846; he looked in this position and identified Neptune the following day, September 24, 1846. In the late 1800s further calculation showed that the orbit of Neptune was also being disturbed by something, so a search was mounted for another distant planet, dubbed planet "X." The search for planet "X" was pioneered by Percival Lowell (1855–1916), who founded the Lowell Astronomical Observatory in Arizona, who unsuccessfully searched the skies for this hypothesized planet from 1905 until his death in 1916. Clyde Tombaugh resumed the search in 1929 and then discovered a planet "X" in the right location on February 18, 1930. The name Pluto was suggested for "planet X" by an 11-year-old girl, Venetia Burney, and the name was adopted by a vote at the Lowell observatory on March 24, 1930. Subsequent studies of Pluto revealed that it was a very small object, and many astronomers argued that it should not be a planet, and could not have such an effect on the orbit of Neptune. In a twist of fate, later observations of the mass of Neptune by the *Voyager 2* spacecraft flyby in 1989 revealed that the mass of Neptune was overestimated by 0.5 percent, and this change was enough to explain the discrepancies in the orbits of Neptune and Uranus that initially led to the search for planet "X" (Pluto). Thus, the very reason for searching for a ninth planet was false.

Pluto is quite different from other planets. Not only is it very small compared to all other planets, but also it orbits far from the plane of the ecliptic, and it resides in the *Kuiper Belt,* along with objects that are about the same order of magnitude in size and mass as Pluto. Enis, an orbiting body further out than the Kuiper Belt in the scattered disk is 27 percent larger than Pluto. Pluto is thought to be composed of 98 percent nitrogen ice, along with methane and carbon monoxide, similar to other objects, including comets, in the Kuiper Belt and in the scattered disk that overlaps with the outer

Origin of Earth by Asteroid Impacts

Although the universe formed about 14 billion years ago, it was not until 5 billion years ago that Earth started forming in a solar nebula, consisting of hot solid and gaseous matter spinning around a central protosun. The solid particles in the nebula coalesced with each other and grew larger and larger, forming a spinning disk of asteroids, dust, comets, and gas. As the solar nebula spun and slowly cooled, large asteroids and edge of the Kuiper Belt. If Pluto were to orbit close to the Sun, it would develop a long cometary tail, and would be classified as a comet, not a planet.

With the advent of more powerful telescopes and data from space missions in the 1980s, 1990s, and 21st century, many objects with masses approaching that of Pluto have been discovered. After much debate and discussion the International Astronomical Union proposed that planets need to be defined on the basis of three main criteria, and on August 24, 2006, adopted the following definition of a planet: "The IAU . . . resolves that planets and other bodies, except satellites, in the solar system be defined into three distinct categories in the following way:

- A planet is a celestial body that (a) is in orbit around the Sun, (b) has sufficient mass for its self-gravity to overcome rigid body forces so that it assumes a hydrostatic equilibrium (nearly round) shape, and (c) has cleared the neighborhood around its orbit.
- A "dwarf planet" is a celestial body that (a) is in orbit around the Sun, (b) has sufficient mass for its self-gravity to overcome rigid body forces so that it assumes a hydrostatic equilibrium (nearly round) shape, (c) has not cleared the neighborhood around its orbit, and (d) is not a satellite.
- All other objects, except satellites, orbiting the Sun shall be referred to collectively as "Small Solar System Bodies."

The International Astronomical Union made some further footnotes to their revised definition of a planet.

- The eight planets are: Mercury, Venus, Earth, Mars, Jupiter, Saturn, Uranus, and Neptune.
- An IAU process will be established to assign borderline objects into dwarf planet and other categories.
- These currently include most of the Solar System asteroids, most Trans-Neptunian Objects (TNOs), comets, and other small bodies.

The IAU further resolved that "Pluto is a 'dwarf planet' by the above definition and is recognized as the prototype of a new category of Trans-Neptunian Objects." Thus, after 100 years of searching for planet "X," and 76 years of imposing as a planet since Pluto's discovery in 1930, the formerly most-distant planet is now regarded as the second largest known dwarf planet in the solar system, and as just another large object in the Kuiper Belt of the outer solar system.

proto-planets including the protoearth formed, sweeping up enough matter by their gravitational attraction to have formed a small proto-planet by 4.6 billion years ago. Materials accreted to the protoearth as they sequentially solidified out of the cooling solar nebula, with the high temperature elements solidifying and accreting first. The early materials to accrete to the proto-planet were rich in iron (which forms solids at high temperatures), whereas the later materials to accrete were rich in hydrogen, helium, and sodium (which form solids at lower temperatures, and would not accrete until the solar nebula cooled). Heat released by gravitational condensation, the impact of late large asteroids, and the decay of short-lived radioactive isotopes caused the interior of Earth to melt, perhaps even forming a magma ocean to a depth of 310 miles (500 km). This melting allowed dense iron and nickel that was accreted during condensation of the solar nebula to begin to sink to the core of the planet, releasing much more heat in the process, and causing more widespread melting. This early differentiation of Earth happened by 4.5 or 4.4 billion years ago, and caused the initial division of Earth into layers including the dense iron-nickel rich core and the silicate rich mantle. The outer layer of Earth was probably a solid crust for most of this time since it would have cooled by conductive heat transfer to the atmosphere and space. The composition of this crust is unknown and controversial, since none of it is known to be preserved.

Between 4.55 and 3.8 billion years ago Earth was bombarded by meteorites, some large enough to severely disrupt the surface, vaporize the atmosphere and ocean, and even melt parts of the mantle. By about 4.5 billion years ago, it appears as if a giant *impactor,* about the size of Mars, hit the protoearth. This impact ejected a huge amount of material into orbit around the protoearth, and some undoubtedly escaped. The impact probably also formed a new magma ocean, vaporized the early atmosphere and ocean (if present), and changed the angular momentum of Earth as it spins and orbits the Sun. The material in orbit coalesced to form the Moon, and the Earth-Moon system was born. Although not certain, this impact model for the origin of the Moon is the most widely accepted hypothesis, and it explains many divergent observations. First, the Moon orbits at 5.1° from the ecliptic plane, whereas Earth orbits at 23.4° from the ecliptic, suggesting that some force, such as a collision, disrupted the angular momentum and rotational parameters of Earth-Moon system. The Moon is retreating from Earth resulting in a lengthening of the day by 15 seconds per year, but the Moon has not been closer to Earth than 149,129 miles (240,000 km). The Moon is significantly less dense than Earth and other terrestrial planets, being depleted in iron and enriched in aluminum, titanium, and other related elements. These relationships suggest that the Moon did not form by accretion from the solar nebula at its present location in the solar system. However, the chemical composition of igneous rocks from the Moon is similar to those from Earth's mantle, suggesting a common origin. The age of the moon rocks shows that it formed at 4.5 billion

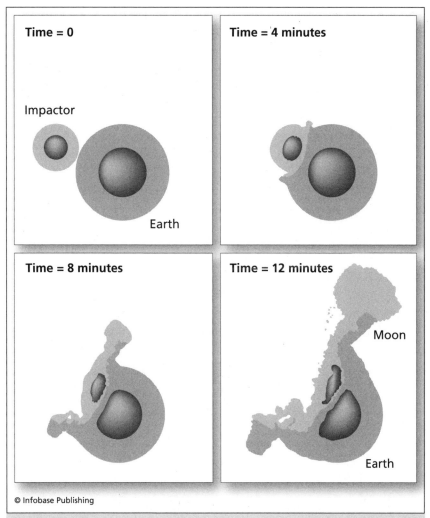

Diagram of Moon origin by giant impact. A Mars-sized object collides with the protoearth about 4.4 or 4.5 billion years ago sending huge amounts of crustal and mantle material into orbit around the Earth, some of which coalesces to form the Moon. *(modified from M. E. Kipp and H. J. Melosh)*

years ago, with some magmatism continuing until 3.1 billion years ago, consistent with the impactor hypothesis.

The atmosphere and oceans of Earth probably formed from early degassing of the interior by volcanism within the first 50 million years of Earth history. It is likely that our present atmosphere is secondary, in that the first or primary atmosphere would have been vaporized by the late great impact that formed the Moon, if it survived being blown away by an intense solar wind when the Sun was in a *T-Tauri stage* of evolution. The primary atmosphere would have been composed of gases left over from accretion, including primarily hydrogen, helium, methane, and ammonia, along with nitrogen, argon, and neon. However, since the atmosphere has much less than the expected amount of these elements, and is quite depleted in these volatile elements relative to the Sun, it is thought the primary atmosphere has been lost to space.

Gases are presently escaping from Earth during volcanic eruptions, and also being released by weathering of surface rocks. The secondary atmosphere was most likely produced from degassing of the mantle by volcanic eruptions, and perhaps also by cometary impact. Gases released from volcanic eruptions include nitrogen, sulfur, carbon dioxide, and water, closely matching the suite of volatiles that comprise the present atmosphere and oceans. However, there was no or little free oxygen in the early atmosphere, as oxygen was not produced until later, by photosynthetic life.

The early atmosphere was dense, with water, carbon dioxide, sulfur, nitrogen, and hydrochloric acid. The mixture of gases in the early atmosphere would have made greenhouse conditions similar to that presently existing on Venus. However, since the early Sun during the *Hadean Era* was approximately 25 percent less luminous than today, the atmospheric greenhouse served to keep temperatures close to their present range, where water is stable, and life can form and exist. As Earth cooled, water vapor condensed to make rain that chemically weathered igneous crust, making sediments. Gases dissolved in the rain made acids, including carbonic acid (H_2CO_3), nitric acid (HNO_3), sulfuric acid (H_2SO_4), and hydrochloric acid (HCl). These acids were neutralized by minerals (which are bases) that became sediments, and chemical cycling began. These waters plus dissolved components became the early *hydrosphere,* and chemical reactions gradually began changing the composition of atmosphere, getting close to the dawn of life.

Life originated on the early Earth during the Hadean, or before 3.8 billion years ago. There are several different options for the initial trigger of life. It is quite possible that life came to Earth on late accreting *planetsimals* (comets) as complex organic compounds, or perhaps it came from interplanetary dust. If true, this would show how life got to Earth, but not how, when, where, or why it originated. Life may also have originated on Earth, in the deep sea near a hydrothermal vent, or in shallow pools with the right chemical mixture. To start, life probably needed an energy source, such as lightning, or perhaps submarine hydrothermal vents, to convert simple organic compounds into building blocks of life (RNA–ribonucleic acid) and amino acids.

Conclusion

The solar system began to form from a spinning solar nebula about 5 billion years ago, 9 billion years after the universe started expanding from nothing in the big bang some 14 billion years ago. This solar nebula consisted of a mass of gas, dust, and fragments that began spinning faster as gravitational forces caused the material to collapse in on itself. Temperatures ranged from extremely hot in inner parts of the solar nebula, to cold in the outer reaches. Planets began accreting by accumulating more and more dust and small fragments to the bigger planetsimals that began rotating around the large mass accumulating as the Sun at the center of the disk, and these early planetsimals grew to proto-planets, still experiencing many impacts with large asteroids and comets by 4.56 billion years ago. As the main planets formed, they differentiated into core-mantle-crust systems, and in the late bombardment period from about 4.5 to 3.5 billion years ago, these planets suffered many impacts with large asteroids and comets. Several large, differentiated bodies in what is now the asteroid belt were destroyed by large impacts, forming billions of fragments that now form the bulk of meteorites that hit Earth. The inner planets are made dominantly of silicate minerals and are called the rocky or terrestrial planets, whereas the outer planets are mainly gaseous, often called the Jovian planets after the largest body, Jupiter. Comets come from further out in the solar system, most from beyond the orbit of Neptune.

2

Orbits and Compositional Classification of Meteorites

Understanding of the composition of meteorites and asteroids has evolved with time. Early studies relied on meteorites, the bodies that had fallen to Earth, since no space travel or observations were possible during the early studies of previous centuries. Recently, space missions to asteroids and remote sensing has enabled observations of asteroids in space to be integrated with the data from samples taken from meteorites collected on Earth.

There is a general increase in ice content in asteroids as the distance from the Sun of their orbits increase. Geologists classified meteorites collected on Earth based on their composition (reflected in the types of minerals present), and in how much they have been metamorphosed, or changed by events that have subjected the meteorites to higher temperatures and pressures. It is clear that many meteorites were part of planetsimals (small planets) that had formed iron-rich cores, and then were probably destroyed in a catastrophic collision with another large asteroid early in the history of the solar system, spreading the asteroid debris of both planetsimals across the solar system. Other asteroids, comets, and meteorites appear not to have ever been parts of larger planets, and may represent some of the primordial matter from the solar nebula from which the solar system formed.

Compositional Classification of Meteorites
Meteorites are classified on the basis of their composition and structure. The aim of such a classification scheme is to group together all the

Photo of iron meteorite from Barringer Meteor Crater, Coconino County, Arizona (a sample weighs 110 g) *(Kenneth V. Pilon; Shutterstock)*

known bodies that may share a common parent body, whether it was a large asteroid, comet, planet, or moon. This is achieved by placing known asteroids into groups and subgroups based on their important mineralogical, physical, chemical, and isotopic properties.

Meteorites are made from material similar to that which makes up Earth, including common silicate minerals, plus iron and nickel metals. Some meteorites also contain small lumps of material called *chondrules* that represent melt droplets that formed before the meteorite fragments were accreted to asteroids, and thus represent some of the oldest material in the solar system. Some meteorites also contain presolar grains, often comprised of tiny carbon crystals in the form of diamonds.

Traditional classification schemes for meteorites broke them into three main groups based on composition. These groups include *stony meteorites* composed mostly of rocky material, *iron meteorites* composed mostly of metallic material, and mixtures called *stony-iron meteorites*. These groups were then divided into subgroups, for instance the stony meteorites were divided into *chondrites* and *achrondrites* based on whether or not they contained chondrules. The iron meteorites were divided into textural groups including structures such as octahedrites, hexahedrites, and ataxites. More recently these textures have not been used for classification but only for descriptive purposes, and the iron meteorites are further divided based on chemistry. Stony-iron meteorites were divided into pallasites and mesosiderites.

More modern classification schemes use a simpler classification, where meteorites are classified as either chondrites or nonchondrites. The nonchrondrites are divided into primitive and differentiated types. The differentiated nonchondrites have three groups, including the achondrites, stony irons, and irons.

It is often difficult to recognize meteorites on Earth, since they have similar minerals to many Earth rocks. Many meteorites develop a fused crust on their surface from the heat during entry through Earth's atmosphere. Most of the meteorites from Earth used for classifications have been collected from Antarctica, where the only place for rocks on the ice fields to come from is from space. Most, about 85 percent of all meteorites falling on Earth are chondrites, thought to represent largely primitive solar material. For the nonchrondrites, many classifications and descriptions are aimed at determining if they come from larger parent bodies that broke up during early impacts, and if so, what the characteristics of this parent body may have been.

CHONDRITES

Chondrites are meteorites that have chemical compositions that are very similar to that of the Sun. Since the Sun comprises about 99 percent of the mass of the solar system, it is assumed that the composition of the Sun is about the average composition for the entire solar system, and that this average composition is about what the original composition of the solar system was when it formed. Therefore, since chondrites and the Sun have similar compositions, chondrites are thought to have very primitive compositions that are close to the average starting material that formed the solar system.

Chondritic meteorites contain small round nodules called chondrules, that are made of a mixture of crystals and glass. Most interpretations for the origin of chondrules suggest that they represent small droplets of liquid that condensed during the earliest stages of the formation of the solar system, before they were incorporated into the meteorites. Chondrules that have been dated yield isotopic ages of 4.568 billion years, the time that the solar system began to condense from the solar nebula. Thus, chondrules represent small remnants of the earliest solar system material. Other chondritic meteorites, such as the famous Allende meteorite, that have been dated also give ages of 4.566 billion years old, very similar to that obtained from the chondrites.

Many experiments have been done on chondrules to determine their exact components and the conditions that they formed under, since they are interpreted to have formed during the early stages of the formation of the solar system. Knowing the conditions of their formation yields information about the conditions in the early solar nebula. Most experiments show that the chondrules formed at temperatures of at least 2,700°F (1,500°C) and that the chondrules cooled rapidly. Some chondrules contain unusual minerals. One group of these contain a group of very high-temperature minerals and is called *calcium-aluminum inclusions* (CAIs), typically exhibiting textures like concentric skins of an onion. Experiments on the temperature of formation of these CAIs indicate that they formed at temperatures of at least 3,100°F (1,700°C), and underwent slow cooling. Based on these extraordinarily high temperatures, it is thought that these CAIs represent the oldest parts of the oldest fragments of the early solar system.

Most chondritic meteorites consist of mixtures of chondrules and the minerals olivine and pyroxene, and show little evidence of being heated or metamorphosed since they formed. Some, however, show textures like partial melting that indicate that they were heated to temperatures of up to 1,800°F (1,000°C) after they formed. Still others are cut by veins that have minerals with water in their structures such as carbonates, sulfates, and magnetite. Thus, water existed in the asteroid belt in the early solar system. It is likely that the range in the amount of heating of chondrites reflects that they were incorporated into a larger body, with the higher temperature heating happening deeper inside this now-destroyed asteroid or proto-planetary body.

Isotopic dating techniques have shown that most chondritic meteorites cooled within 60 million years of the time of the formation of the solar system. At some time after that, impacts in the asteroid belt broke the larger proto-planets or asteroid parent bodies into smaller pieces now preserved as the asteroid belt. Some chondrites are composed of strongly fragmented rock called *breccia*, produced by these early collisions in the asteroid belt. Calculations of the pressures needed to produce these breccias indicate that the pressures reached 75 Giga Pascals, or the equivalent of 750,000 times the atmospheric pressure on Earth.

Chondritic meteorites are divided into a number of classes with similar compositions and textures, thought to represent formation in similar parts of the solar system. These in turn are divided into groups that are thought to represent fragments of the same parent body.

The main classes of chondrites include the ordinary chondrites, carbonaceous chondrites, and enstatite chondrites. Some classifications add further subdivisions based on the type of alteration or metamorphism, such as alteration by water, or metamorphism by late heating. Ordinary chondrites are thought to have formed in parent bodies that were 100–120 miles (165–200 km) in diameter. *Carbonaceous chondrites* contain organic material such as hydrocarbons in rings and chains, and amino acids. Even though these are organic molecules, and can be building blocks of life, no life has been found on any meteorites, unless they were contaminated on Earth. Enstatite chondrites contain small sulfide minerals that indicate very rapid cooling, suggesting that the original material was from deep in a larger body that was broken apart by strong impacts, and the deep material cooled quickly in space after the violent collisions. The enstatite chondrites typically have impact breccias in their structures.

ACHONDRITES

Achondrite meteorites resemble typical igneous rocks found on Earth. They formed by crystallizing from a silicate magma and are remnants of larger bodies in the solar system that were large enough to undergo differentiation and internal melting. These meteorites do not contain chondrules or remnant pieces of the early solar system since they underwent melting and recrystallization.

Some achondrites have been shown to have origins on Earth's Moon and on Mars. They formed by crystallization from magma on these bodies, and were ejected from the gravitational fields of these bodies during large impact events. The debris from these impacts then floated in space until they were captured by the gravitational field of Earth, where they fell as meteorites. These meteorites are named for the places they have fallen on Earth, and include shergottites, nakhlites, and chassignites (collectively named *SNC meteorites* after these three falls). SNC achondrites have ages between 150 million and 1.3 billion years, billions of years younger than other meteorites and the age of the solar system. These ages mean that the SNC meteorites must have come from a large planet that was able to remain hot and sustain magma for a considerable time after formation at 4.56 billion years ago. Chemical analysis of the SNC meteorites revealed that most match the bulk chemistry of Mars, confirming the link. Analysis of the damage done to the surface of these meteorites by cosmic rays as they were in space has yielded further estimates that the time of transit from the ejection during impact on Mars to the landing on Earth is less than 2 million years. Thus, most of the SNC meteorites originated from meteorite impacts on Mars in the past 1–20 million years. It is estimated that about a billion tons of material has landed on Earth that was originally ejected by meteorite impact on Mars. A smaller number of SNC meteorites have been shown to come from Earth's Moon.

Other achondrites formed on other bodies that have been destroyed by giant impacts. The howardites, eucrites, and diogenites are thought to have formed in one body, the largest remnant of which is the asteroid 4 Vesta currently orbiting the Sun in the asteroid belt. The eucrites and diogenites represent basaltic magma that was produced on this early proto-planet, and was destroyed by a large impact at 4.4 billion years ago, within a hundred million years of the formation of the solar system. Eucrites are basalts that contain the minerals clinopyroxene and plagioclase, diogenites contain orthopyroxene that formed layers of dense crystals called cumulates, and howardites are breccias of these rocks that formed during the giant impact that destroyed the parent achondrite body.

There are a number of unusual achondrites that have no known parent bodies. These include the acapulcoites, angrites, brachinites, lodranites, and urelites. Some of these are relatively primitive—for instance, the urelites formed early in the solar system evolution, were heated inside a large parent body and crystallized at 2,300°F (1,250°C), were destroyed in a massive impact then cooled at 50°F (10°C) per hour in the cold vacuum of space. One arubite shows a remarkably fast cooling rate of 1,800°F (980°C) per hour, probably coming from deep within the parent body then being suddenly frozen in space. Brachinites show some of the earliest igneous activity known from any asteroid body, showing the earliest time at which planets may have begun accreting in the early solar system. The crystallized magmas from these bodies have given ages of 4.564 billion years, meaning that the accretion of planetsimals to a size that could partially melt, from the solar nebula happened within 5 million years.

IRON METEORITES

Iron meteorites consist of iron and 5–20 percent nickel, some minor metals, and contain almost no silicate minerals. They are thought to represent the differentiated cores of large planetsimals or proto-planets that formed in the early solar system in the asteroid belt, grew large enough to partially melt and differentiate into core and mantle and crust, then were broken apart by large impacts exposing the core material to outer space. Iron meteorites therefore represent valuable samples of the cores of planetary bodies.

Iron meteorites are famous for exhibiting a crisscross texture known as the *Widmannstatten texture* best shown on polished metallic surfaces. This is produced by intergrown blades of iron and nickel minerals, and the size of the blades is related to the cooling rate of the minerals. The slower the cooling, the larger the crystals grow, so it is possible to calculate the cooling rate of the early planetsimals using the Widmannstatten texture, and from that infer the size of the early planetsimals. A range of different cooling rates and sizes have been determined, ranging from 210°F (100°C) per hour in a body less than 48 miles (80 km) in diameter, to cooling at 9°F (5°C) per year in a body up to 210 miles (340 km) in diameter. Just like the chondrites, the iron meteorites are estimated to have formed into the parent bodies or planetsimals within 5 million years of the formation of the solar system. Additional analysis of the cosmic ray interaction of the surfaces of the iron meteorites can tell the amount of time that they have been exposed and traveling through space. In this case, the exposure age, dating from the time of breakup of the parent body to the time the meteorites fell to Earth, is remarkably different from other meteorites. The iron meteorite parent bodies apparently broke up by impacts only between 200 million and 1 billion years ago, and thus, had survived as large bodies in the asteroid belt for 3.5 to 4.5 billion years.

Iron meteorites are divided into groups on the basis of their textures, and how the iron and nickel minerals are intergrown, and the sizes of the crystals. The names of the main groups include octahedrites, hexahedrites, and ataxites. They are further divided into a large number of classes based on their chemical characteristics, which indicate that they formed in at least several different parent bodies.

STONY IRON METEORITES

As the name implies, stony iron meteorites consists of mixtures of metal and silicate (rocky) components, resembling a cross between achondrites and iron meteorites. They are thought to come from the part of a planetsimal or parent body near the boundary of the core and mantle, incorporating parts of each in the meteorite.

Stony iron meteorites are classified into pallasites and mesosiderites. Pallasites contain a mixture of Widmannstatten-textured iron phases, and large yellow to green olivine crystals, formed along the core-mantle boundary of the parent body. Mesosiderites consist of silicate minerals with inclusions of iron that melted in the core of the parent body. Mesosiderites are puzzling, because the silicate phases are magmatic rocks that formed near the surface of the parent body, and the iron phases are melts from the core of the body. Ages for mesosiderites range from 4.4 to 4.56 billion years old, so they formed early in the history of the solar system. Some models suggest that they are breccias from bodies that only partially differentiated in the planetsimal forming stages of the solar system. These bodies broke up by impact 4.2 billion years ago, then apparently were reassembled by gravity within 10–170 million years. The parent body for the mesosiderites was between 120–240 miles (200–400 km) in diameter.

Orbits and Location of Asteroids in the Solar System

Asteroids have been named and numbered in the order they were discovered, since the first discovery of asteroid 1 Ceres in 1801. Most of the large asteroids are located in the main asteroid belt between Mars and Jupiter, and are thought to have originated by numerous collisions between about 50 large planetsimals in the early history of the solar system. In this belt, the large number of relatively large bodies meant that there were many mutual collisions, and they never coalesced into a single large body like the other planets. There are 33 asteroids known with diameters larger than 120 miles (200 km), and 1,200 known with diameters larger than 19 miles (30 km). The largest is 1 Ceres (590 miles, or 960 km), and the other large asteroids in this belt include 2 Pallas (350 miles; 570 km), 4 Vesta (326 miles; 525 km), 10 Hygiea (279 miles; 450 km), 15 Eunomia (169 miles; 272 km), and Juno (150 miles; 240 km).

Like planets, asteroids orbit the Sun and rotate on their axes, although many asteroids have more of a tumbling motion than the spinning typical of planets. Many asteroids have unusual shapes, and it is not unusual for asteroids to resemble familiar objects, like giant dog-bones (216 Kleopatra, 135 miles; 217 km long) tumbling through space. Typical periods of rotation (corresponding to the length of a day) range from 3 hours to several Earth days, with most falling around periods of 9 hours. Many asteroids are really collections of blocks of rubble all rotating in the same place. These are thought to be asteroids that were once single solid masses, but were strongly fractured and broke apart while in orbit.

Significant Asteroids

NUMBER	NAME	DIAMETER (MILES [KM])	DISCOVERER, LOCATION	DATE
1	Ceres	577 × 596 (930 × 960)	G. Piazzi, Palermo	1801
2	Pallas	354 × 326 × 300 (570 × 525 × 482)	H. W. Olbers, Bremen	1802
3	Juno	150 (240)	K. Harding, Lilienthal	1804
4	Vesta	326 (525)	H. W. Olbers, Bremen	1807
5	Astraea	74 (119)	K. L. Hencke, Driesen	1845
6	Hebe	114 (185)	K. L. Hencke, Driesen	1847
7	Iris	126 (203)	J. R. Hind, London	1847
8	Flora	84 (135)	J. R. Hind, London	1847
9	Metis	114 (184)	A. Graham, Markee	1848
10	Hygiea	279 (450)	A. de Gasparis, Naples	1849
15	Eunomia	169 (272)	A. de Gasparis, Naples	1851
243	Ida	36 × 14 (58 × 23)	J. Palisa, Vienna	1884
433	Eros	21 × 8 × 8 (33 × 13 × 13)	G. Witt, Berlin	1898
951	Gaspra	12 × 7 × 7.5 (19 × 12 × 11)	G. N. Neujmin, Simeis	1916

NUMBER	NAME	DIAMETER (MILES [KM])	DISCOVERER, LOCATION	DATE
1566	Icarus	0.9 (1.4)	W. Baade, Palomar	1949
1862	Apollo	1 (1.6)	K. Reinmuth, Heidelberg	1932
2062	Aten	0.6 (0.9)	E. F. Helin, Palomar	1976
2060	Chiron	111 (180)	C. T. Kowal, Palomar	1977
3554	Amun	1.6 (2.5)	C. S. and E. M. Shoemaker, Palomar	1986
78433	Gertrudolf	(?)	S. F. Honig, Palomar	2002

Inner Solar System Asteroids

There are relatively few asteroids that orbit inside the orbit of Jupiter, since the numerous planets and proximity to the Sun in this region exert many forces that cause the orbits of bodies to become unstable. Most asteroids that end up orbiting in the inner solar system are deflected there by collisions in the other asteroid belts, and have short lifetimes before they impact a planet, are pulled into the Sun, or deflected back to outer space.

Despite these forces there are a couple of places in the inner solar system where gravitational physics lets asteroids have stable orbits. These stable orbits, called *resonances,* are an effect of the gravity and different orbital periods of the larger planets in the inner solar system. Some locations (the resonances) are at stable locations for bodies that orbit at specific rates relative to the larger planets. The largest planet, Jupiter, forms several resonances within which there are many asteroids orbiting, generally known as Jovian asteroids. These include the Trojans, which have an orbital period that is equal to Jupiter's, another group known as the Hildas which orbit 3 times for every 2 orbits of Jupiter, and the Thule asteroids, which orbit 4 times for every three orbits of Jupiter. Just as the resonances represent stable places for asteroids to orbit, the gravitational forces of large planets such as Jupiter cause some places to be particularly unstable for asteroids. These places are devoid of asteroids, and are known as Kirkwood gaps (after their discoverer, Daniel Kirkwood (1814–95), who first described them in 1886).

Gravitational physics results in some additional locations that represent stable orbits for asteroids in the inner solar system. These stable orbits were first described by the French mathematician Joseph-Louis Lagrange (1736–1813) in the late 18th century. Lagrange was able to show that for a two body system (like the Sun and a large planet, like Jupiter) there are five orbital positions inside the orbit of the planet where the gravitational pull of the two large bodies is equal to the centripetal force acting on other bodies between them, and that the two forces cancel each other and make these stable orbits. Three of the five Lagrange orbits turn out to be unstable over long geological time periods, but two yield long-term stable orbits for asteroids. These two Lagrange points turn out to be in the orbit of the planet, located 60 degrees ahead and 60 degrees behind the position of the planet. Asteroids in the solar system that are located in these points are called Trojans, and many asteroids in the inner solar system fall into this category. Trojans exist for the Sun-Jupiter gravitational system, for the Sun-Mars system, and many other planets in the solar system. The most abundant Trojans are orbiting in synchroneity with Jupiter, then with Mars, on either side of the main asteroid belt. The Sun-Earth system has dense concentrations of dust at the Trojan points but no known asteroids.

Gravitational physics predicts that there are two main stable regions in the inner solar system where many asteroids may exist with stable orbits for long periods of time. The first location is inside the orbit of Mercury, but no asteroids have yet been identified in this region. Asteroids that may be in this region are named Vulcan objects, but have proven difficult to observe because of their proximity to the Sun. The second large stable region for asteroids in the inner solar system is known as the main belt, divided into several sub-belts, between the orbits of Mars and Jupiter.

Main Asteroid Belt

By far the largest number of asteroids in the inner solar system are located in the main asteroid belt between the orbits of Mars and Jupiter.

View of the asteroid 243 Ida produced as a mosaic of five image frames acquired by the *Galileo* spacecraft's solid-state imaging system at ranges of 1,900 to 2,375 miles (3,057 to 3,821 km) on August 28, 1993, about 3.5 minutes before the spacecraft made its closest approach to the asteroid *(NASA JPL)*

There are estimated to be between 1.1 and 2 million asteroids in this belt with diameters greater than half a mile (1 km), comprising about 95 percent of the known asteroids. There are probably billions of objects in this belt with diameters of less than half a mile (1 km). Despite the large number of objects in the main asteroid belt, the total mass of all asteroids in this belt is less than one tenth of one percent of the mass of Earth, and represents a mass less than Earth's Moon.

In 1993, the *Galileo* spacecraft flew about 1,500 miles (2,400 km) from asteroid Ida at a relative velocity of 28,000 mph (12.4 km/sec), in the second encounter of an asteroid by a spacecraft. At the time of nearest pass, the asteroid and spacecraft were 274 million miles (441 million km) from the Sun, as illustrated in the photomosaic on this page. Ida is about 32 miles (52 km) in length, more than twice as large as Gaspra, the first asteroid observed by *Galileo* in October 1991. Ida is an irregularly shaped asteroid placed by scientists in the S class (believed to be like stony or stony iron meteorites). It is a member of the Koronis family, presumed fragments left from the breakup of a precursor asteroid in a catastrophic collision. It has numerous craters, including many degraded craters larger than any seen on Gaspra. The extensive cratering dispels theories about Ida's surface being geologically youthful.

The main asteroid belt is located between 1.7 to 4 AU from the Sun, in an unusually large gap, between the planets of Mars and Jupiter. Early models for this gap and the asteroids suggested that perhaps there was once a planet in this gap, but that it was destroyed by a tremendous impact, resulting in the formation of the asteroids. Some of the asteroids obviously come from once-larger objects, since they have metallic material that comes from a differentiated core of a planetlike body, and these differentiated cores need a planet of at least a few hundred miles (few hundred km) to form. However, it is now clear that the huge gravitational forces from Jupiter are so large that they would have prevented a large planet from ever forming in that gap. Instead, new models for most of these asteroids is that some formed a number of several-hundred-mile- (several hundred km-) diameter planetsimals, but that none ever reached true planet size. These planetsimals then repeatedly crashed into each other, forming the numerous and odd shaped fragments in the belts. There are other asteroids in the main asteroid belt that have compositions that show that they were never part of larger bodies, and that they represent material that is "left over" from the solar nebula, still floating freely in space. One of the classes of asteroids, known as carbonaceous chondrites, show unmetamorphosed (never heated or put under high pressure) minerals, showing that they were never deep in a planetary interior, and never located next to the Sun. The compositions of the main belt asteroids shows that they formed in about the same region they are located in with respect to distance from the Sun.

There are several belts of asteroids within the main asteroid belt, and these show variations with distance from the Sun, thought to represent variations in the original solar nebula, and in the different parent bodies that broke up during formation of the solar system. One of the main differences is that asteroids inside 2.5 AU have no water in them, whereas beyond 2.5 AU, the asteroids have water, increasing with distance from the Sun. Not coincidentally, the planets inside the asteroid belt are rocky, whereas those outside the belt are gaseous and icy.

The innermost group of asteroids in the main belt, just beyond the orbit of Mars at 1.52 AU are the Hungaria objects, orbiting between 1.78 and 2.0 AU. These are followed outward by the Flora family between 2.1 and 2.3 AU, then the main part of the main asteroid belt between 2.3 and 3.25 AU. The Koronis asteroids are located in this main section of the main belt, including more than 200 identified large bodies orbiting around 3 AU. A gap lies outward of the Koronis asteroids, then the

Cybele family asteroids orbit the Sun at a distance of 3.5 AU, with properties suggesting they originated from a single large planetsimal that was destroyed early in the history of the solar system. The outermost part of the main asteroid belt is occupied by the Hilda asteroids, orbiting in a resonance from Jupiter at 3.9 to 4.2 AU. Beyond the Hilda family is a gap, followed by the orbit of Jupiter and its Trojans.

Aten, Apollo, and Amor Class Asteroids

In addition to the stable belts, there are numerous asteroids in the inner solar system that have unstable orbits, and these bodies present the greatest threat to Earth and its inhabitants. Some of these asteroids have orbits that cross the paths of other planets, including Earth, and pose an even greater risk of impact. These asteroids are classified according to their distance from the Sun.

Aten asteroids orbit less than one *astronomical unit* (AU, the distance from the Sun to Earth) and an orbital period of less than one year, and some of these cross Earth's orbit. There are more than 220 known Aten objects, many of which are being tracked as they pose a high risk of impact with Earth. *Apollo asteroids* are similar to Atens in that they cross Earth's orbit, except they have periods longer than one year. Of the more than 1,300 known Apollo asteroids, the largest is 1685 Toto, which is 7.5 miles (12 km) across. Collision of this object with Earth would be cataclysmic. There are more than 13 Apollo asteroids known with diameters greater than three miles (5 km), any of which is larger than the asteroid that hit Earth at the end of the Cretaceous, killing the dinosaurs and causing a mass extinction event. Another class of inner planet-crossing asteroids are the *Amors,* which orbit between Earth and Mars, but do not cross Earth orbit. There are more than 1,200 known Amor objects, and the moons of Mars (Deimos and Phobos) may be Amors that were gravitationally captured by Mars.

The asteroid that is deemed the most threatening to Earth (among known objects) is 4179 Toutatis. This asteroid is a mile (1.6 km) across and orbiting in a plane only one half a degree different from Earth's. Remembering that the asteroid that hit Chicxulub and killed the dinosaurs was only six miles (10 km) across, the devastation potential of a collision of Earth with Toutatis is collosal. The possibility of a collision is not that remote—on September 29, 2004, Toutatis passed by Earth at only four times the distance to the Moon. The next largest object in nearly coplanar orbits with Earth are less than 0.6 miles (1 km) in diameter, but a collision with these would also produce an impact crater greater than

15 miles (25 km) across. Impact statistics predict that objects this size should still be hitting Earth three times per million years.

Outer Solar System Asteroids

The outer solar system, beyond the orbit of Jupiter, is awash in asteroids, most of which are icy compared to the rocky and metallic bodies of the inner solar system. In addition to the Trojans around Jupiter, a group of about 13,000 asteroids with highly eccentric and inclined orbits cross the path of Jupiter, in positions that cause relatively frequent collisions and deflections of the asteroids into the inner solar system. Asteroids whose orbits are inside the orbit of a planet generally do not hit that planet, but only planets closer to the Sun than its orbit. This is an artifact of the great gravitational attraction of the Sun, constantly pulling these objects closer in toward the center of the solar system.

Centaurs are a group of asteroids with orbits that have highly eccentric orbits that extend beyond yet cross the orbits of Jupiter and Saturn, thus can potentially collide with these planets. Many of these are large bodies that are thought to have been deflected inward from the Kuiper Belt, into unstable orbits that have them on an eventual collision course with the giant planets, or to be flung into the inner solar system. Coming from so far out in the solar system Centaurs are icy bodies. One Centaur, Chiron, is about 50 miles (85 km) in diameter, is classified as a minor planet and exhibits a cometary tail when it is at its perihelion but not along other parts of its orbit. Chiron therefore is classified as both an asteroid and a comet.

Trans-Neptunian objects are a class of asteroid that orbit beyond the orbit of Neptune at 30 AU, and beyond into the Kuiper Belt, extending from 30-49 AU. Beyond the Kuiper Belt, there is a gap of about 11 AU of relatively few asteroids before the beginning of the *Oort Cloud.* The total number of objects in this belt is unknown but undoubtedly large, as many are being discovered as the ability to detect objects at this distance increases. More than a thousand Trans-Neptunian objects are currently documented.

Kuiper Belt

The Kuiper Belt contains many rocky bodies, and is thought to be the origin of many short period comets. However, few of the known Kuiper Belt objects have been shown to have frozen water, but may have ices of other compositions. The total mass of asteroids in the Kuiper Belt is estimated at about 20 percent of Earth's mass, about 100 times as much as the mass of the main asteroid belt.

Formerly classified as a planet, Pluto, and its moon Charon, are Kuiper Belt objects. Pluto is one of the larger Kuiper Belt objects, but its size is not anomalous for the belt—there are thought to be thousands of Kuiper Belt objects with diameters greater than 600 miles (1,000 km), 70,000 asteroids or comets with diameters greater than 60 miles (1,000 km), and half a million objects with diameters greater than 30 miles (50 km). Saturn's moon Phoebe is an icy captured asteroid that was deflected inward from the Kuiper Belt, and gravitationally captured by Saturn. Its surface shows a mixture of dusty rock debris and ice.

Oort Cloud

The Oort Cloud is a roughly spherical region containing many comets and other objects, extending from about 60 AU to beyond 50,000 AU, or about 1,000 times the distance from the Sun to Pluto, or about a light-year. This distance of the outer edge of the solar system is also about one quarter of the way to the closest star neighbor, Proxima Centauri. The Oort Cloud is thought to be the source for long-period comets and Halley-type comets that enter the inner solar system. It contains rocky as well as icy bodies.

The Oort Cloud can be divided into two main segments including the inner, doughnut-shaped segment from 50–20,000 AU, and the outer spherical shell extending from 20,000 to at least 50,000 AU. Some estimates place the outer limit of the Oort Cloud at 125,000 AU. The inner part of the Oort Cloud is also known as the Hills Cloud, and is thought to be the source of Halley-type comets, whereas the outer Oort Cloud is the source of the long-period comets that visit the inner solar system. The Hills, or Inner Oort Cloud contains much more material than the outer Oort Cloud, yet the outer cloud contain trillions of comets and bodies larger than .8 mile (1.3 km) across, spaced tens of millions of miles (km) apart. The total mass of the outer Oort Cloud is estimated to be several Earth masses.

Short- and Long-Period Comets

Comets are bodies of ice, dust, and rock that orbit the Sun, and exhibit a coma (or atmosphere) extending away from the Sun as a tail when they are close to the Sun. They have orbital periods that range from a few years, to a few hundred and even thousands of years. Short-period

Selected Kuiper Belt and Oort Cloud Objects in Approximate Size Order

OBJECT	APPROXIMATE DIAMETER (MILES [KM])	FRACTION OF PLUTO'S DIAMETER	DISCOVERY AND COMMENTS
2003 UB313	2,100 (3,360)	1.4	Mike Brown, Chad Trujillo, and David Rabinowitz; though there is uncertainty in the measurement of the diameter, the body is certainly larger than Pluto
Pluto	1,486 (2,390)	1.0	Clyde Tombaugh, 1930. Since 2006, Pluto is no longer regarded as a planet.
Sedna (2003 VB$_{12}$)	~1,000 (~1,600)	0.6 to 0.7	Mike Brown; may be the first object found in the Oort cloud
2004 DW	~1,000 (~1,600)	0.6 to 0.7	Mike Brown and Chad Trujillo; plutino
50000 Quaoar (2002 LM$_{60}$)	780 (1,250)	0.52	Chad Trujillo and Mike Brown; cubewano
Charon	730 (1,170)	0.49	James Christy and Robert Harrington, 1978
20000 Varuna (2000 WR$_{106}$)	~620 (~1,000)	0.4	Robert S. MacMillan, Spacewatch project; cubewano
55565 (2002 AW$_{197}$)	~590 (~950)	0.4	Chad Trujillo and Mike Brown; cubewano
55636 (TX$_{300}$)	~590 (~950)	0.4	Jet Propulsion Laboratory NEAT program. 2002; cubewano
28978 Ixion (2001 KX$_{76}$)	~580 (~930)	0.4	Lawrence Wasserman and colleagues at the Deep Ecliptic Survey; plutino
1999 CL$_{119}$	~270 (~430)	0.2	Most distant object in the Kuiper Belt (perihelion 46.6 AU, no other perihelion farther); cubewano
15760 (1992 QB$_1$)	150 (240)	0.1	David Jewitt and Jane Luu; the definitive cubewano and first discovered Kuiper Belt object

Note: Diameters marked as approximate (~) may have errors as large as 125 miles (200 km).

comets are those with orbital periods of less than 200 years, and most of these orbit in the plane of the ecliptic in the same direction as the planets. Their orbits take them past the orbit of Jupiter at *aphelion,* and near the Sun at *perihelion.* Long-period comets have highly elongated or eccentric orbits, with periods longer than 200 years and extending to thousands or perhaps even millions of years. These comets range far beyond the orbits of the outer planets, although they remain gravitationally bound to the Sun. Another class of comets are called single-apparition comets, meaning that they have a hyperbolic trajectory that sends them past the inner solar system only once, then they are ejected from the solar system.

Before late 20th-century space probes collected data on comets, comets were thought to be composed primarily of ices and to be lone wanderers of the solar system. Now, with detailed observations, it is clear that comets and asteroids are transitional in nature, both in composition and orbital character. Comets are now known to consist of rocky cores with ices around them or in pockets, and many have an organic-rich dark surface. Many asteroids are also made of similar mixtures of rocky material with pockets of ice. There are so many rocky/icy bodies in the outer solar system in the Kuiper Belt and Oort Cloud, that comets are now regarded as the most abundant type of bodies in the universe. It is thought that there may be one trillion comets in the solar system, of which only about 3,350 have been cataloged. Most are long-period comets, but several hundred short period comets are known as well.

The heads of comets can be divided into several parts, including the *nucleus,* the *coma,* or gaseous rim that the tail extends from, and a diffuse cloud of hydrogen. The heads of comets can be quite large, some larger than moons, or objects including Pluto (see table on page 30). Most cometary nuclei are between 0.3–30 miles (0.5–50 km) in diameter, and consist of a mixture of silicate rock, dust, water ice, and other frozen gases such as carbon monoxide, carbon dioxide, ammonia, and methane. Some comets are known to contain a variety of organic compounds including methanol, hydrogen cyanide, formaldehyde, ethanol, and ethane, as well as complex hydrocarbons and amino acids. Although some have many organic molecules, no life is known from comets. These organic molecules make cometary nuclei into some of the darkest objects in the universe, reflecting only 2–4 percent of the light that falls on their surfaces. This dark color may actually help comets absorb heat, promoting the release of gases to form the tail.

Cometary tails can change in length, and can be 80 times larger than head when the comet passes near the Sun.

As the comet approaches the Sun it begins to emit jets of ices consisting of methane, water, and ammonia, and other ices. It is thought that the tails form when the radiation from the Sun cracks the crust of the comet, and begins to vaporize the volatiles like carbon, nitrogen, oxygen, and hydrogen, carrying away dust from the comet in the process. The mixture of dust and gases emitted by the comet then forms a large but weak atmosphere around the comet, called the coma. The radiation and solar wind from the Sun causes this coma to extend outward away from the Sun forming a huge tail. The tail is complex and consists of two parts—the gases released from the comet form an ion tail that gets elongated in a direction pointing directly away from the Sun, and may extend along magnetic field lines for more than 1 AU (9,321,000 miles; 150,000,000 km), and the coma from which the tail extends may become larger than the Sun. Dust released by the comet forms a tail with a slightly different orientation, forming a curved trail that follows the orbital path of the comet around the Sun.

Photo of comet Hyakutake, April 1996, showing a tail extending away from the Sun *(Photo Researchers)*

Short-period comets originate in the Kuiper Belt, whereas long-period comets originate in the Oort Cloud. Many comets are pulled out of their orbits by gravitational interactions with the Sun and planets, or by collisions with other bodies. When these events place comets in orbital paths that cross the inner solar system, these comets may make close orbits to the Sun, and may also collide with planets including Earth.

Several space missions have recently investigated the properties of comets. These include *Deep Space 1*, which flew by Comet Borrelly in 2001. Comet Borrelly is a relative small comet, about five miles (8 km) at its longest point, and the mission showed that the comet consists of asteroidlike rocky material, along with icy plains from which the dust jets that form the coma were being emitted. In 1999 NASA launched the *Stardust Comet Sample Return* Mission, which flew through the tail of comet Wild 2 and collected samples of the tail in a silica gel, and returned them to Earth in 2006. Scientists were expecting to find many particles of interstellar dust, or the extrasolar material that the solar nebula was made of, but instead found little of this material, and predominantly silicate mineral grains of Earthlike solar system composition. The samples collected revealed that comet Wild 2 is made of a bizarre mixture of material that includes some particles that formed at the highest temperatures in the early solar system, and some particles

Selected Comets			
NAME	ORBITAL PERIOD (YEARS)	NEXT PERIHELION DATE	ORBITAL ECCENTRICITY	ORBITAL INCLINATION (DEGREES)
1P Halley	76.01	2061	0.967	162.2
2P Encke	3.30	2007	0.847	11.8
6P d'Arrest	6.51	2008	0.614	19.5
9P Tempel 1	5.51	2005	0.519	10.5
19P Borrelly	6.86	2008	0.624	30.3
26P Grigg-Skjellerup	5.09	2008	0.664	21.1
55P Tempel-Tuttle	32.92	2031	0.906	162.5
75P Kohoutek	6.24	2007	0.537	5.4
81P Wild 2	6.39	2010	0.540	3.2
95P Chiron	50.70	2046	0.38	7.0
107P Wilson-Harrington	4.30	2005	0.622	2.8
Hale-Bopp	4,000	~4,400	0.995	89.4
Hyakutake	8,000–14,000	~42,000	0.9998	124.9

that formed at the coldest temperatures. To explain this, scientists have suggested that the rocky material that makes up the comet formed in the inner solar system during the early history of the solar system, and were then ejected to the outer bounds of the solar system beyond the orbit of Neptune, where the icy material was accreted to the comet. Calcium-Aluminum Inclusions, that represent some of the oldest, highest temperature parts of the early solar system were also collected from the comet. One of the biggest surprises was the capture of a new class of organic material from the comet tail. These organic molecules are more primitive than any on Earth, and from any found in any meteorites, and are known as polycyclic aromatic hydrocarbons. Some samples even contain alcohol. These types of hydrocarbons are thought to exist in

DID LIFE COME TO EARTH ON A COMET?

Comets are rich in water, carbon, nitrogen, and complex organic molecules that originate deep in space from processes of radiation induced chemistry. Many of the organic molecules in the coma of comets originated in the dust of the solar nebula at the time and location where the comets initially formed in the early history of the solar system. Comets are relatively small bodies that have preserved these early organic molecules in a cold, relatively pristine state. This has led many scientists to speculate that life may have come to Earth on a comet, early in the history of the planet. It is clear that comets both delivered organic material to the early Earth, and also destroyed and altered organic material with the heat and shock from impacts. Numerical models of the impact of organic-rich comets with Earth show that some of the organic molecules could have survived the force of impact. The organic molecules in comets may be the source of the prebiotic molecules that led to the origins of life on Earth.

Studies of the chemistry and origin of the atmosphere and oceans suggest that the entire atmosphere, ocean, and much of the carbon on Earth, including that caught up in carbonate rocks like limestone, originated from cometary impact. The period of late impacts of comets and meteorites on Earth lasted about a billion years after the formation of Earth, before greatly diminishing in intensity. Life on Earth began during this time, hinting at a possible link between the transport of organic molecules to Earth by comets, and the development of these molecules into life. However, the early atmosphere of Earth was also carbon dioxide–rich (much of which came from comets), and organic synthesis was also occurring on Earth.

In addition to bringing organic molecules to Earth, the energy from impacts certainly destroyed much of any early biosphere that attempted to establish itself on the early Earth. Even the late, very minor K-T impact at Chicxulub had major repercussions to life on Earth—certainly, the late bombardment phase in the early history of Earth that was characterized by many very large impacts would have had a more profound effect on life. It is likely that any life that established itself on Earth would need to be sheltered from the harsh surface environment, perhaps finding refuge along the deep sea volcanic systems known as black smokers, where temperatures remained hot but stable, and nutrients in the form of sulfide compounds were used by early organisms for energy.

interstellar space, and may yield clues about the origin of water, oxygen, carbon, and even life on Earth.

Origin of Asteroids, Meteorites, and Comets

The asteroid belt is thought to have originated as a group of larger planetsimals that began to be formed within 5 million years of the formation of the solar system, and that soon after this the planetsimals began to be broken apart by mutual collisions between these early planetsimals. Some collisions happened within a few tens to hundreds of millions of years after initial formation of the bodies, whereas others have happened within the past 200 million years. Most of these collisions are induced by the gravitational forces between Jupiter and the Sun.

The composition of asteroids is determined through remote sensing methods, typically using reflection spectra from the surfaces of asteroids. Presently no samples have been returned from exploration missions to asteroids, so it is difficult to directly correlate their composition with meteorites.

The remote sensing studies of asteroids reveal that they have a diverse range of compositions, and match closely the range of meteorite compositions found on Earth. In this way, some meteorites have been matched to remnants of their parent bodies in the asteroid belt. For instance, asteroid 4 Vesta has the same composition as and is thought to be the largest remnant of the parent body for the howardite, eucrite, and diogenite classes of achondrites.

There is a gradual change in the composition of asteroids with distance from the Sun. The asteroids closest to Mars are classified as S-type silicate bodies, and resemble ordinary chondrites. These are followed outward by more abundant B- and C-types, containing some water-rich minerals and appear to be carbonaceous chondrites. D- and P-types rise in abundance outward, but these do not have any known correlatives in meteorites that have fallen to Earth. These are dark objects, and appear rich in organic material.

The outer solar system asteroids, including the Oort Cloud, are thought to be the remnant of the original proto-planetary disc that the solar system formed from 4.6–4.5 billion years ago. Many of the objects in the Oort Cloud may have initially been closer to the Sun, but moved outward from gravitational perturbations by the outer planets. The current mass of the Oort Cloud, 3–4 Earth masses, is much less than the 50–100 Earth masses estimated to have been ejected from the solar system during its formation. It is possible that the outer edges of the

Oort Cloud interact gravitationally with the outer edges of other Oort Clouds from nearby star systems, and that these gravitational interactions cause comets to be deflected from the cloud into orbits that send them into the inner solar system.

Bombardment of Earth by comets early in its history may have brought large quantities of water, and organic molecules, to the planet. In some models for the evolution of the early Earth, most of the volatiles that were initially on the planet were blown away by a strong solar wind associated with a T-Tauri phase of solar evolution, and the present day atmosphere and oceans were brought to Earth by comets. Small microcomets continue to bombard Earth constantly, bringing a constant stream of water molecules to Earth from space.

Conclusion

Modern classification schemes for meteorites divide them into either chondrites or nonchondrites. The nonchrondrites are divided into primitive and differentiated types. The differentiated nonchondrites have three groups, including the achondrites, stony irons, and irons. These groups are based on the chemistry and texture of the meteorites, and reflect their origin. Chondrites have compositions that are similar to the Sun, and represent the average composition of the solar system, thought to be close to the original composition of the solar nebula. Many chondrites contain chondrules, which are small, originally liquid melt drops of the original material that condensed to form the solar system 4.6 billion years ago. Some chondrites contain materials called calcium-aluminum inclusions, that may represent pre-solar system material. One class of chondrites, called carbonaceous condrites, contain complex organic molecules. The variation in chondritic meteorites is thought to represent formation at different depths in a large, 100–120-mile- (165–200-km-) wide asteroid that was destroyed in a catastrophic collision early in the history of the solar system, dispersing the fragments across the solar system.

The nonchrondrites are divided into primitive and differentiated types. The differentiated nonchondrites have three groups, including the achondrites, stony irons, and irons. Achondrites are rocky silicate igneous rocks, whereas the irons consist of mixtures of iron and nickel. Stony irons represent a transitional group. These meteorites are also thought to have formed in several parent bodies that were destroyed by collisions in what is now the asteroid belt, but that these bodies were initially large enough (120–240 miles (200–400 km)) across, that they were able to differentiate into crust, mantle, and core. The irons are from the core of these bodies, the achondrites from the mantle and crust, and the stony irons from the transition zone. Some achondrites are unusual, and have been shown to have been ejected from the Moon and Mars during impacts, eventually landing on Earth.

Most meteorites are thought to come from the asteroid belt, where 1 to 2 million asteroids with diameters greater than 0.6 miles (1 km) are orbiting the Sun between Mars and Jupiter. They may get pushed into Earth-crossing orbits after being deflected by collisions in the asteroid belt or by gravitational perturbations during complex orbital dynamics. Spectral measurements of some of the asteroids show that they have compositions that correlate with the meteorites sampled on Earth, and a crude gradation of compositions in the asteroid belt is thought to represent both the original distribution of different parent bodies that broke up during collisions, and the initial compositional trends across the solar nebula. Asteroids closer to the Sun are rockier, with more silicates and metals, whereas those further out have more ices of nitrogen, methane, and water.

There are several different groups of asteroids that have unstable orbits that cross the paths of the planets in the inner solar system. These objects represent grave dangers to life on Earth, as any impacts with large objects are likely to be catastrophic. These Earth and Mars orbit-crossing asteroids are classified based on their increasing distance from the Sun into Aten, Apollo, and Amor class asteroids. Some of these asteroids are being tracked, to monitor the risk to life on Earth, since collisions of asteroids of this size are known to cause mass extinction events, such as the Cretaceous-Tertiary extinction that killed the dinosaurs. Major impacts occur on Earth about every 300,000 years.

The outer solar system also hosts belts of asteroids, and the number and mass of these objects pales the amount of material in the inner solar system. There are many names for asteroids and other bodies that are orbiting in specific regions, but the bodies of most significance include the Trans-Neptunian objects that orbit beyond the orbit of Neptune at 30 AU and into the Kuiper Belt, that extends to about 49 AU. Beyond this there is a relatively empty gap before the beginning of the Oort Cloud at 60 AU. Most objects in the Kuiper Belt and the Oort Cloud are bodies that consist of mixtures of rock and ice, and are the source region for comets. There are thought to be thousands of Kuiper Belt objects with diameters greater than 600 miles (1,000 km), 70,000 asteroids or comets with diameters greater than 60 miles (1,000 km), and half a million objects with diameters greater than 30 miles (50 km).

The Oort Cloud represents the outer reaches of the solar system, and may actually extend into the Oort Cloud of the nearby star system, Proxima Centauri. There are thought to be trillions of comets in the Oort Cloud over 0.8 miles (1.3 km) in diameter, totally several Earth masses. The Oort Cloud is the source of long-period comets, with orbits longer than 200 years. Comets typically have a rocky core, and emit jets of ices consisting of methane, water, and ammonia, and other ice compounds. Many comets are coated by a dark surface, consisting of complex organic molecules, and these may be the source for much of the carbon and volatile elements on Earth that presently make up much of the atmosphere and ocean. Some scientists speculate that comets may be responsible for bringing the complex organic molecules to Earth that served as the building blocks for life.

3

Meteorite and Comet
Impacts with Earth

There is ample evidence that many small and some large meteorites have hit Earth frequently throughout time. Several hundred impact craters have been recognized to be preserved on continents, and a few have been recognized on the ocean floor. There is a wide range in the way these craters appear. Some are small, only a few yards (m) across, such as the small ca. 5,000-year-old craters at Henbury in the Northern Territories of Australia, to others that are up to hundreds of miles (hundreds of km) across, such as the Precambrian Vredefort dome in South Africa. Eyewitness accounts describe many events such as fireballs in the sky recording the entry of a meteorite into Earth's atmosphere, to the huge explosion over Tunguska, Siberia, in 1908 that leveled thousands of square miles (km) of trees, and created atmospheric shock waves that traveled around the world. Many theories have been proposed for the Tunguska event, the most favored of which is the impact of a comet fragment with Earth. Fragments of meteorites are regularly recovered from places like the Antarctic ice sheets, where rocky objects on the surface have no place to come from but space. Although meteorites may appear as flaming objects moving across the night skies, they are generally cold icy bodies when they land on Earth, and only their outermost layers get heated from the deep freeze of space during their short transit though the atmosphere.

Most meteorites that hit Earth originate in the asteroid belt, situated between the orbits of Mars and Jupiter. There are at least a million asteroids in this belt with diameters greater than 0.6 miles (1 km), 1,000 with diameters greater than 19 miles (30 km), and 200 with diameters greater than 62 miles (100 km). These are thought to be either remnants of a small planet that was destroyed by a large impact event, or perhaps fragments of rocky material that failed to coalesce into a planet, probably due to the gravitational effects of the nearby massive planet of Jupiter. Most scientists favor the second hypothesis, but recognize that collisions between asteroids have broken apart from a large body to expose a planetlike core and mantle now preserved in the asteroid belt.

Other objects from space may collide with Earth. Comets are masses of ice and carbonaceous material mixed with silicate minerals that are thought to originate in the outer parts of the solar system, in a region called the Oort Cloud. Other comets have a closer origin, in the Kuiper Belt just beyond the orbit of Neptune. There is considerable debate that small icy Pluto, long considered the small outermost planet,

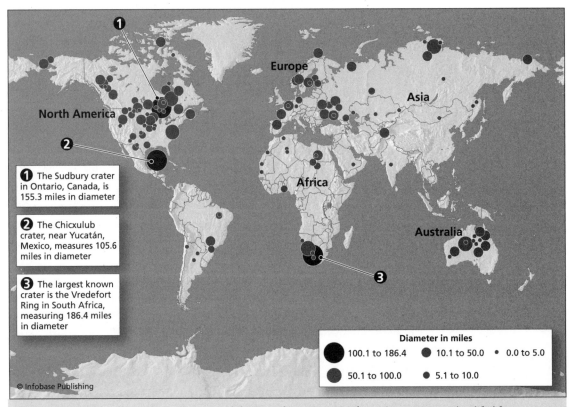

Map of world showing known impact craters, with larger circles representing larger impact craters *(modified from Geological Survey of Canada)*

has been reclassified as a large Kuiper Belt object (see page 8). Comets may be less common near Earth than meteorites, but they still may hit Earth with severe consequences. There are estimated to be more than a trillion comets in our solar system. Since they are lighter than asteroids, and have water-rich and carbon-rich compositions, many scientists have speculated that cometary impact may have brought water, the atmosphere, and even life to Earth.

Selected Terrestrial Impact Craters				
CRATER NAME	STATE/PROVINCE	COUNTRY	DIAMETER (MILES [KM])	APPROXIMATE AGE (MILLIONS OF YEARS)
Vredefort		South Africa	190 (300)	2020
Sudbury	Ontario	Canada	150 (250)	1850
Chicxulub	Yucatán	Mexico	110 (180)	65
Manicougan	Quebec	Canada	60 (100)	214
Popigai		Russia	60 (100)	35
Acraman	South Australia	Australia	55 (90)	450
Chesapeake Bay	Virginia	U.S.	53 (85)	35
Puchezh-Katunki		Russia	50 (80)	175
Morokweng		South Africa	44 (70)	145
Kara		Russia	40 (65)	73
Beaverhead	Montana	U.S.	38 (60)	625
Tookoonooka	Queensland	Australia	34 (55)	130
Charlevoix	Quebec	Canada	34 (54)	360
Kara-Kul		Tajikistan	33 (52)	within 5 Myr of present
Siljan		Sweden	33 (52)	368
Montagnais	Nova Scotia	Canada	28 (45)	50

Inventory of Impact Craters on Earth

Impact craters are known from every continent including Antarctica. Several hundred impact craters have been mapped and described in detail by geologists, and some patterns about the morphology, shape, and size of the craters have emerged from these studies. The most obvious variations in crater style and size are related to the size of the impacting meteorite, but other variations depend on the nature of the bedrock or cover, the angle and speed of the impact, and what the impactor was—whether rock or ice. Impacts are known from all ages, and are preserved at various states of erosion and burial, allowing study of the many different levels of cratering, and a better understanding of the types of structures and rocks produced during impacts.

Impact Cratering Mechanics and Consequences

The collision of meteorites with Earth produces impact craters, which are generally circular bowl-shaped depressions. There are more than 200 known impact structures on Earth, although processes of weathering, erosion, volcanism, and tectonics have undoubtedly erased many thousands more. The moon and other planets show much greater densities of impact craters, and since Earth has a greater gravitational pull than the moon, it should have been hit by many more impacts than the moon.

Meteorite impact craters have a variety of forms but are of two basic types. Simple craters are circular bowl-shaped craters with overturned rocks around their edges, and are generally less than three miles (5 km) in diameter. They are thought to have been produced by impact with objects less than 100 feet (30 m) in diameter. Examples of simple craters include the Barringer Meteor Crater in Arizona, and Roter Kamm in Namibia. Complex craters are larger, generally greater than two miles (3 km) in diameter. They have an uplifted peak in the center of the crater, and have a series of concentric rings around the excavated core of the crater. Examples of complex craters include Manicougan, Clearwater Lakes, and Sudbury in Canada; Chicxulub in Mexico; and Gosses Bluff in Australia.

The style of impact crater depends on the size of the impacting meteor, the speed at which it strikes the surface, and to a lesser extent the underlying geology and the angle at which the meteor strikes Earth. Most meteorites hit Earth with a velocity between 2.5 and 25 miles per second (4–40 km/sec), releasing tremendous energy when they hit. Meteor Crater in Arizona was produced about 50,000 years ago by a meteorite approximately 100 feet (30 m) in diameter that hit the desert in Arizona, releasing the equivalent of 4 *megatons* (3.6 megatonnes) of

Formation of a Meteorite Crater

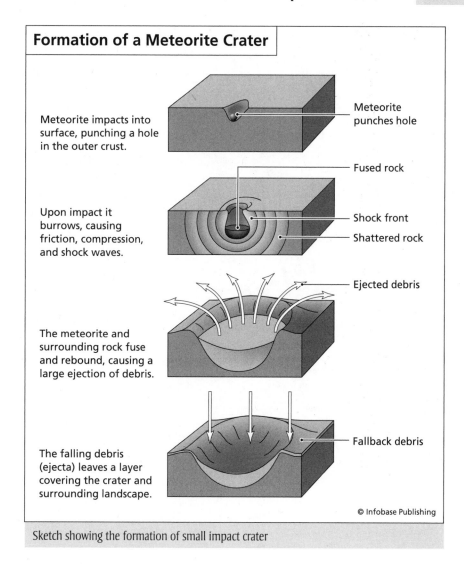

Meteorite impacts into surface, punching a hole in the outer crust.

Meteorite punches hole

Fused rock

Upon impact it burrows, causing friction, compression, and shock waves.

Shock front

Shattered rock

Ejected debris

The meteorite and surrounding rock fuse and rebound, causing a large ejection of debris.

The falling debris (ejecta) leaves a layer covering the crater and surrounding landscape.

Fallback debris

© Infobase Publishing

Sketch showing the formation of small impact crater

TNT. The meteorite body and a large section of the ground at the site were suddenly melted by shock waves from the impact, which released about twice as much energy as the eruption of Mount Saint Helens. Most impacts generate so much heat and shock pressure that the entire meteorite and a large amount of the rock it hits are melted and vaporized. Temperatures may exceed thousands of degrees in a fraction of a second as pressures increase a million times atmospheric pressure during passage of the shock wave. These conditions cause the rock at the site of the impact to accelerate downward, outward, and then the ground rebounds and tons of material are shot outward and upward into the atmosphere.

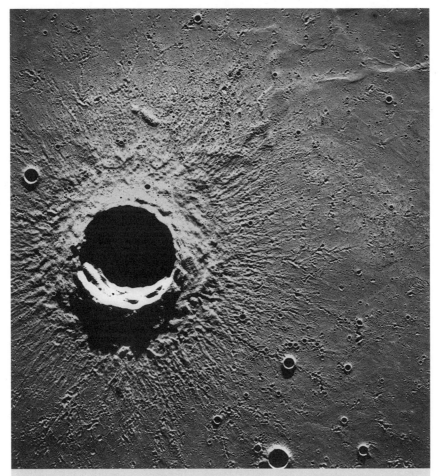

Photo showing Crater Timocharis on the Moon, photographed from *Apollo 15*, 1971, 20 miles (32 km) wide, with large uplifted rim and radiating bands of ejecta *(Photo Researchers)*

Impact cratering is a complex process. When the meteorite strikes it explodes and vaporizes, and sends shock waves through the underlying rock, compressing the rock and crushing it into breccia, and ejecting material (conveniently known as *ejecta*) back up into the atmosphere, from where it falls out as an ejecta blanket around the impact crater. Large impact events may melt the underlying rock forming an impact melt, and may form distinctive minerals that only form at exceedingly high pressures.

After the initial stages of the impact crater forming process, the rocks surrounding the excavated crater slide and fall into the deep hole, enlarging the diameter of the crater, typically making it much wider than it is deep. Many of the rocks that slide into the crater are brecciated or otherwise affected by the passage of the shock wave, and may preserve these effects as brecciated rocks, high pressure mineral phases, shatter cones, or other deformation features.

Impact cratering was probably a much more important process in the early history of Earth than it is at present. The flux of meteorites from most parts of the solar system was much greater in early times, and it is likely that impacts totally disrupted the surface in the early Precambrian. At present the meteorite flux is about a hundred tons (91 tonnes) per day (somewhere between 10^7–10^9 kg/yr), but most of this material burns up as it enters the atmosphere. Meteorites that are about a tenth of an inch to several feet (mm–m) in diameter make a flash of light (a shooting star) as they burn up in the atmosphere, and the

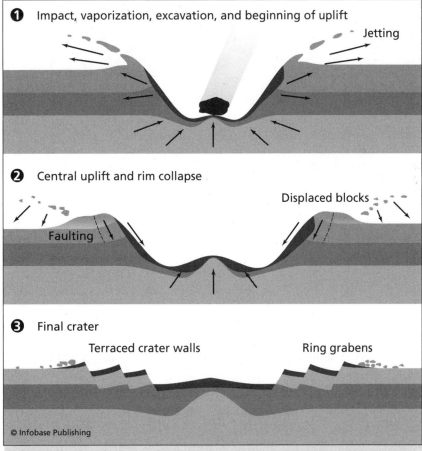

Sketch of a large impact crater, showing how the impactor excavates a large crater, vaporizes, and then the crater rim collapses, forming a series of terraced crater walls and central uplift.

Photo example of complex impact crater on the Moon. This oblique view shows the International Astronomical Union (IAU) Crater 302 on the Moon surface, photographed by the *Apollo 10* astronauts in May 1969. Note the terraced walls of the crater and central cone. Center point coordinates are located at 162 degrees, 2 minutes east longitude and 10 degrees, 1 minute, south latitude *(NASA)*

remains fall to Earth as a tiny glassy sphere of rock. Smaller particles, known as cosmic dust, escape the effects of friction and slowly fall to Earth as a slow rain of extraterrestrial dust.

Meteorites must be greater than three feet (1 m) in diameter to make it through the atmosphere without burning up from friction. Earth's surface is currently hit by about one small meteorite per year. Larger impact events occur much less frequently, with meteorites 300 feet (90 m) in diameter hitting once every 10,000 years, 3,000 feet (900 m) in diameter hitting Earth once every million years, and six miles (10 km) in diameter hitting every 100 million years. Meteorites of only several hundred feet (hundreds of m) in diameter could create craters about one mile (1–2 km) in diameter, or if they hit in the ocean, they would generate tsunami more than 15 feet (5 m) tall over wide regions. The statistics of meteorite impact show that the larger events are the least frequent.

Tunguska, Siberia, June 30, 1908

On June 30, 1908, a huge explosion rocked a very remote area of central Siberia centered near the Podkamennaya (Lower Stony) Tunguska River, in an area now known as Krasnoyarsk Krai in Russia. After years of study and debate it is now thought that this huge explosion was produced by fragment of Comet Encke that broke off the main body, and exploded in the air about six miles (10 km) above the Siberian Plains.

The early morning of June 30, 1908, witnessed a huge, pipelike fireball moving across the skies of Siberia, until at 7:17 A.M. a tremendous explosion rocked the Tunguska area and devastated more than 1,160 square miles (3,000 square km) of forest. The force of the blast is estimated to have been equal to 10–30 megatons (9.1–27 megatonnes), and is thought to have been produced by the explosion, six miles (10 km) above the surface of Earth, of an asteroid or comet with a diameter of 200 feet (60 m). The energy equivalence of this explosion was close to 2,000 times the energy released during the explosion of the Hiroshima atomic bomb. More energy was released in the air blast than the impact and solid earthquakes, demonstrating that the Tunguska impacting body exploded in the air. The pattern of destruction reflects the dominance of atmospheric shock waves rather than solid earthquakes that are estimated to have been about a magnitude 5 earthquake. Atmospheric shock waves were felt thousands of miles away, and people located closer than 60 miles (100 km) from the site of the explosion were knocked unconscious, and some were thrown into the air by the force of the explosion. Fiery clouds and deafening explosions were heard more than 600 miles (965 km) from Tunguska.

For a long time, one of the biggest puzzles at Tunguska was the absence of an impact crater, despite all other evidence that points to an impact origin for this event. It is now thought by many scientists that a piece of a comet, Comet Encke, broke off the main body as it was orbiting nearby Earth, and this fragment entered Earth's atmosphere and exploded about five to six miles (8–10 km) above the Siberian plains at Tunguska. This model was pioneered by Slovakian astronomer L'ubor Kresák (1927–94), following earlier suggestions by the British astronomer F. J. W. Whipple (1876–1943) in the 1930s that the *bolide* (a name for any unidentified object entering the planet's atmosphere) at Tunguska may have been a comet. Other scientists suggest the bolide may have been a meteorite, since comets are weaker than metallic or stony meteorites, and more easily break up and explode in the atmosphere before they hit Earth's surface. If the Tunguska bolide was a comet, it likely would have broken up higher in the atmosphere. In either case, calculations show that, because of the rotation of Earth, if the impact explosion happened only 4 hours and 47 minutes later, the city of Saint Petersburg (Leningrad) would have been completely destroyed by the air blast. Air blasts from disintegrating meteorites or comets the size of the Tunguska explosion occur about once every 300 years on Earth, whereas smaller explosions, about the size as the nuclear bombs dropped on Japan, occur in the upper atmosphere about once per year.

EYEWITNESS ACCOUNTS OF THE TUNGUSKA EXPLOSION, JUNE 30, 1908

Few people lived in the core region of the Tunguska explosion in 1908. There were however many eyewitness accounts from places near the edges of the core damage zone, and from other places as far as Australia and Scandinavia and the United Kingdom. The first published report of the explosion was in the Irkutsk City newspaper on July 2, 1908, published two days after the explosion, as related below:

> . . . the peasants saw a body shining very brightly (too bright for the naked eye) with a bluish-white light. . . . The body was in the form of "a pipe," i.e., cylindrical. The sky was cloudless, except that low down on the horizon, in the direction in which this glowing body was observed, a small dark cloud was noticed. It was hot and dry and when the shining body approached the ground (which was covered with forest at this point) it seemed to be pulverized, and in its place a loud crash, not like thunder, but as if from the fall of large stones or from gunfire was heard. All the buildings shook and at the same time a forked tongue of flames broke through the cloud. All the inhabitants of the village ran out into the street in panic. The old women wept, everyone thought that the end of the world was approaching.

S. B. Semenov, an eyewitness from the village of Vanovara, located about 37 miles (60 km) south of the explosion site, described the event as follows:

> . . . I was sitting in the porch of the house at the trading station of Vanovara at breakfast time . . . when suddenly in the north . . . the sky was split in two and high above the forest the whole northern part of the sky appeared to be covered with fire. At that moment I felt great heat as if my shirt had caught fire; this heat came from the north side. I wanted to pull off my shirt and throw it away, but at that moment there was a bang in the sky, and a mighty crash was heard. I was thrown to the ground about three sajenes (about 23 feet, or 7 m) away from the porch and for a moment I lost consciousness. . . . The crash was followed by noise like stones falling from the sky, or guns firing. Earth trembled, and when I lay on the ground I covered my head because I was afraid that stones might hit it.

Local Inuit people reported the blast, as the following testimony from Chuchan, of the Shanyagir Tribe recorded by ethnographer I. M. Suslov in 1926:

All the trees in the Siberian forest in an area the size of a large city were leveled by the explosion of Tunguska, which was fortunately unpopulated at the time. However, a thousand reindeer belonging to the Evenki people of the area were reportedly killed by the blast. The pattern of downed trees indicates that the projectile traveled from the southeast to the northwest as it exploded. The height of the explosion over Tunguska is about the optimal height for an explosion-induced air burst to cause maximum damage to urban areas, and it has been calculated that

---

We had a hut by the river with my brother Chekaren. We were sleeping. Suddenly we both woke up at the same time. Somebody shoved us. We heard whistling and felt strong wind. Chekaren said, "Can you hear all those birds flying overhead?" We were both in the hut, couldn't see what was going on outside. Suddenly, I got shoved again, this time so hard I fell into the fire. I got scared. Chekaren got scared too. We started crying out for father, mother, brother, but no one answered. There was noise beyond the hut, we could hear trees falling down. Chekaren and I got out of our sleeping bags and wanted to run out, but then the thunder struck. This was the first thunder. Earth began to move and rock, wind hit our hut and knocked it over. My body was pushed down by sticks, but my head was in the clear. Then I saw a wonder: trees were falling, the branches were on fire, it became mighty bright, how can I say this, as if there was a second sun, my eyes were hurting, I even closed them. It was like what the Russians call lightning. And immediately there was a loud thunderclap. This was the second thunder. The morning was sunny, there were no clouds, our Sun was shining brightly as usual, and suddenly there came a second one!

Chekaren and I had some difficulty getting out from under the remains of our hut. Then we saw that above, but in a different place, there was another flash, and loud thunder came. This was the third thunder strike. Wind came again, knocked us off our feet, struck against the fallen trees.

We looked at the fallen trees, watched the tree tops get snapped off, watched the fires. Suddenly Chekaren yelled "Look up" and pointed with his hand. I looked there and saw another flash, and it made another thunder. But the noise was less than before. This was the fourth strike, like normal thunder.

Now I remember well there was also one more thunder strike, but it was small, and somewhere far away, where the Sun goes to sleep.

All of these observers report a generally similar sequence of events, from different perspectives. The bolide formed a giant, columnlike fireball that moved from southeast to northwest across the Siberian sky, then exploded in several pieces high above the ground surface, with audible to deafening sounds, and scorching to noticeable heat. The explosions were followed by the air blast that moved down in the center of the area, then outward toward the edges of the blast zone. These eyewitness accounts provide scientists with some of the best observation of airbursts of this magnitude, and serve as a valuable lesson in the behavior of meteorites or asteroids that explode before hitting the surface.

if the area was heavily populated at the time of the impact that at least 500,000 people would have died. Despite the magnitude and significance of this event, the Tunguska region was very remote, and no scientific expeditions to the area to investigate the explosion were mounted until 1921, 13 years after the impact, and even then the first expedition only reached the fringes of the affected area. The first scientific expedition was led by a geologist named Leonid Kulik (1883–1942), who was looking for meteorites along the Podkamennaya–Tunguska River basin, and he heard stories from the local people of the giant explosion that happened in 1908, and that the explosion had knocked down trees, blown roofs off huts, and knocked people over and even caused some people to go deaf from the noise. Kulik then convinced the Russian government that an expedition needed to be mounted into the remote core of the Tunguska blast area, and this expedition reached the core of the blast zone in 1927. Kulik and his team found huge tracts of flattened and burned trees, but were unable to locate any impact crater.

In June 2007, a team of scientists from the University of Bologna suggested that a small lake named Lake Cheko, located about five miles (8 km) from the epicenter of the blast, may be the impact site. Other scientists challenge this interpretation, noting that the lake has thick sediments, implying an older age than the age of the impact.

The atmospheric blast from the Tunguska explosion raced around the planet two times before diminishing. Residents of Siberia who lived within about 50 miles (80 km) of the blast site reported unusual glowing light coming from the sky for several weeks after the explosion. It is possible that this light was being reflected by a stream of dust particles that were ripped off a comet as it entered the atmosphere before colliding with Earth's surface. The unusual nighttime illumination was reported from across Europe and western Russia, showing the extent of the dust stream in the atmosphere.

As the fireball from the Tunguska airburst moved through the atmosphere, the temperatures at the center of the fireball were exceedingly hot, estimated to be 30 million degrees Fahrenheit (16.6 million Celsius). On the ground, trees were burned and scorched, and silverware utensils in storage huts near the center of the blast zone were melted by the heat. After the impact leveled the trees for a distance of about 25

Opposite: Maps of Tunguska, showing (a) the areal extent across which the fireball from the impact in 1908 was sighted, and (b) the huge area across which the trees of the Siberian forest were knocked down by the impact

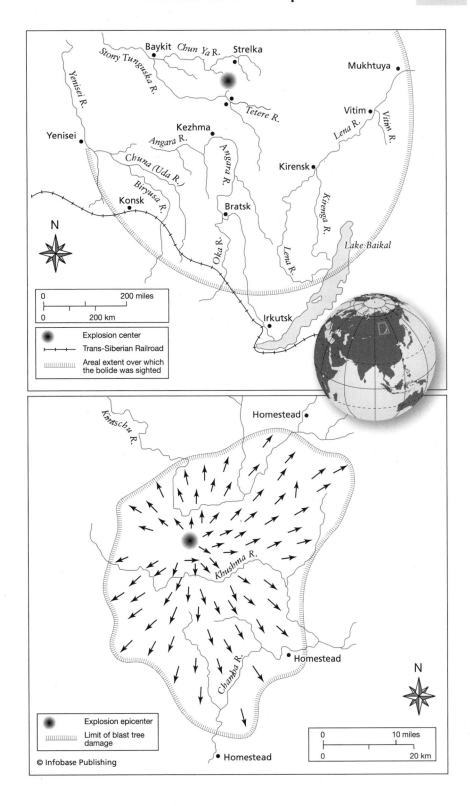

miles (40 km) around the center of the impact, forest fires ravaged the area, but typically only burned the outer surface of many trees, as if the fires were a short-lived flash of searing heat.

The type of body that exploded above Tunguska has been the focus of much speculation and investigation. One of the leading ideas is that the impact was caused by a comet that exploded in the atmosphere above Tunguska, a theory pioneered by F. J. W. Whipple in a series of papers from 1930–34. In the 1960s small silica and magnetite spherules that represent melts from an extraterrestrial source were found in soil samples from Tunguska, confirming that a comet or meteorite had exploded above the site. Further analysis of the records of the airblast indicated that there were several pressure waves recorded by the event. The first was the type associated with the rapid penetration of an object into the atmosphere, and at least three succeeding bursts recorded the explosions of a probably fragmented comet about six miles (10 km) above the surface.

There have been other reported explosions, or possible explosions, of meteorites above the surface of Earth, creating air blasts since the Tunguska event, although none has been as spectacular. On August 13, 1930, a body estimated to be about 10 percent the size of the Tunguska bolide exploded above the Curuçá River in the Amazonas area in Brazil, but documentation of this event is poor. On May 31, 1965, an explosion with the force equivalent of 600 tons (544 tonnes) of TNT was released eight miles (13 km) above southeastern Canada, and approximately 0.4 ounces (1 gram) of meteorite material was recovered from this event. Similar sized events, also thought to be from meteorite explosions at about eight miles (13 km) above the surface, were reported from southeast Canada on May 31, 1965, and over Lake Huron (Michigan) on September 17, 1966, and over Alberta Canada on February 5, 1967. No meteorite material was recovered from any of these events. Two mysterious explosions, probably meteorites exploding with an equivalent to about 25 tons (23 tonnes) of TNT, were reported, strangely, over the same area of Sassowo, Russia, on April 12, 1992, and July 8, 1992. A larger explosion and airburst, estimated to be equivalent to 10,000 tons of TNT, was reported over Lugo, Italy, on January 19, 1993, and another 25 ton (23 tonne) event over Cando, Spain, on January 18, 1994. Russia was struck again, this time in the Bodaybo region, by a 500–5,000 ton (450–4,500 tonne) equivalent blast on September 25, 2002, after a 26,000 ton (23,600 tonne) airburst from a meteorite explosion was recorded over the Mediterranean between Greece and Libya. The last reported airburst was from a high-altitude explosion, 27 miles (43 km) over Snohomish, Washington, on June 3, 2004. Clearly, airbursts associated with the explosion of meteorites or comets are fairly common events, just events as strong as the Tunguska explosion only happen about once every 300 years.

Barringer Crater, Arizona

One of the most famous and visited impact craters in the United States is the Barringer Meteor Crater in Arizona, and is the first structure that was almost universally accepted by the scientific community as a meteorite impact structure. The crater is .75 miles (1.2 km) across, and has an age of 49,000 years before present. However, this acceptance did not come easy. The leading proponent of the meteorite impact model was Daniel Barringer (1860–1929), a mining company executive, who argued for years against the powerful head of the U.S. Geological Survey, Grove K. Gilbert (1843–1922), who argued that the crater was a volcanic feature. For years, Daniel Barringer was losing the argument because in his model the crater should have been underlain by a massive iron-nickel deposit from the meteorite, which was never found,

Photo of Barringer Meteor Crater, Coconino County, Arizona. The rim of the crater is composed of overturned rocks excavated from inside the crater by the impact. *(Visuals Unlimited)*

since the meteorite was vaporized by the heat and energy of the impact. However, by 1930 enough other evidence for the origin of the crater had been accumulated to convince the scientific community of its origin by impact from space.

Barringer Crater is a small crater, and has a roughly polygonal outline that is partly controlled by weak zones (fractures and joints) in the underlying rock. The bedrock of the area is simple, consisting of a cover of alluvium, underlain by the thin Triassic Moenkopi sandstone, about 300 feet (90 m) of the Permian Kaibab limestone, and 900 feet (270 m) of the Permian Coconino sandstone. The rim of the crater is 148 feet (45 m) higher than the surrounding desert surface, and the floor of the crater lies 328 feet (100 m) lower than the surrounding average desert elevation. The rim of the crater is composed of beds of material that originally filled the crater, and were thrown or ejected out during the impact process. The beds in the rim rocks are fragmented and brecciated, and the whole sequence that was in the crater is now lying upside down on the rim. The underlying beds are turned upward as the crater is approached, reflecting this powerful bending and overturning that occurred when the interior rocks were thrown onto the rim by the impact.

Although the large mass of iron and nickel that Daniel Barringer sought at the base of the crater does not exist, thousands of small meteorite fragments have been collected from around the outer rim of the crater, as from as far away as four miles (7 km) from the crater. The soil around the crater, for a distance of up to six miles (10 km) is pervaded by meteorite dust, suggesting that the impacting meteorite was vaporized upon impact, and the debris settled around the crater in a giant dust cloud. Estimates of the size of the meteorite that hit based on the amount of meteorite debris found are about 12,000 tons (10,884 tonnes).

There are many other indicators of the impact origin of Meteor crater. The widespread brecciation or fragmentation of the rim, and presence of iron-rich shale from weathering of the meteorite, is consistent with an impact origin. More importantly, there are high-temperature glasses and minerals preserved that form during the high pressures of meteorite impact. In some places the rock has been melted into *impact glasses* that require shock pressures and temperatures. Some very rare minerals that only form at very high pressures have been found at Barringer Crater. These include high-pressure phases of quartz known as coesite and stishovite, and also small diamonds formed by high pressures associated with the impact.

Chicxulub Impact and the Cretaceous-Tertiary Mass Extinction

The geologic record of life on Earth shows that there have been several sudden events that led to the extinction of large numbers of land and marine species in a very short interval of time, and many of these are thought to have been caused by the impact of meteorites with Earth. Many of the boundaries between geologic time periods have been selected based on these mass extinction events. Some of the major mass extinctions include that between the Cretaceous and Tertiary Periods, marking the boundary between the Mesozoic and Cenozoic Eras. At this boundary, at 66 million years ago, dinosaurs, ammonites, many marine reptile species, and a large number of marine invertebrates suddenly died off, and the planet lost about 26 percent of all biological families and numerous species. At the boundary between the Permian and Triassic Periods (which is also the boundary between the Paleozoic and Mesozoic eras) 245 million years ago, 96 percent of all species became extinct. Many of the hallmark life-forms of the Paleozoic era were lost, including the rugose corals, trilobites, many types of brachiopods, and marine organisms including many foraminifer species. There are several other examples of mass extinctions, including one at the boundary between the Cambrian and Ordovician Periods at 505 million years ago, where more than half of all families disappeared forever.

These mass extinctions have several common features that point to a common origin. Impacts have been implicated as the cause of many of the mass extinction events in Earth history. The mass extinctions seem to have occurred on a geologically instantaneous time scale, with many species present in the rock record below a thin clay-rich layer, and dramatically fewer species present immediately above the layer. In the case of the Cretaceous-Tertiary extinction, some organisms were dying off slowly before the dramatic die-off, but a clear sharp event occurred at the end of this time of environmental stress and gradual extinction. Iridium anomalies have been found along most of the clay layers, considered by many to be the "smoking gun" indicating an impact origin as the cause of the extinctions. One half million tons (454,000 tonnes) of iridium are estimated to be in the Cretaceous-Tertiary boundary clay, equivalent to the amount that would be contained in a meteorite with a six-mile (10-km) diameter. Other scientists argue that volcanic processes within Earth can produce iridium, and impacts are not necessary. Still other theories about the mass extinctions and loss of the dinosaurs exist, including that they died off from disease, insect bites, and genetic evolution that led to a great dominance of male over female species. However, other rare elements and geochemical anomalies are present along the Cretaceous-Tertiary boundary, supporting the idea that a huge meteorite hit Earth at this time, and was related in some way to the extinction of the dinosaurs, no matter what else may have been contributing to their decline at the time of the impact.

Other features have been found that support the impact origin for the mass extinctions. One of the most important is the presence of some high-pressure minerals formed at pressures not reachable in the outer layers of Earth. The presence of the high-pressure mineral equivalents of quartz, including coesite, stishovite, and an extremely high-pressure phase known as diaplectic glass strongly implicates an impacting meteorite, which can produce tremendous pressures during the passage of shock waves related to the force of the impact. Many of the clay layers associated with the iridium anomalies also have layers of tiny glass spherules, which are thought to be remnants of melted rock produced during the impact that were thrown skyward where it crystallized as tiny droplets that rained back on the planet's surface. They also have abundant microdiamonds similar to those produced during meteorite impact events. Layers of carbon-rich soot are also associated with some of the impact layers, and these are thought to represent remains of global wildfires that were

Model of Allosaurus dinosaur, from the Late Jurassic period *(Science Photo Library)*

Photo of ammonite fossil Acantoplites, Cretaceous period *(Shutterstock)*

ignited by the impacts. Finally, some of the impact layers also record huge tsunamis that swept across coastal regions.

Many of these features are found around and associated with an impact crater recently discovered on Mexico's Yucatán Peninsula. The Chicxulub Crater is about 66 million years old and lies buried half beneath the waters of the Gulf of Mexico, and is half on land. Tsunami deposits of the same age are found in inland Texas, much of the Gulf of Mexico, and the Caribbean, recording a huge tsunami perhaps several hundred feet (hundred m) high that was generated by the impact. The crater is at the center of a huge field of scattered spherules that extends across Central America and through the southern United States. It is a large structure, and is the right age to be the crater that records the impact at the Cretaceous-Tertiary boundary, recording the extinction of the dinosaurs and other families.

The discovery and documentation of the meteorite crater on the Yucatán Peninsula, near the town of Chicxulub (meaning tail of the devil) was a long process, but the crater is now widely regarded as the one that marks the site of the impact that caused the Cretaceous-Tertiary (K-T) mass extinction, including the loss of the dinosaurs. The crater was first discovered and thought to be an impact crater in the 1970s by Glen Penfield, who was working on oil exploration, and did not publish his results, but presented some ideas for the impact origin of the structure in some scientific meetings in the 1980s. In 1981, a geology student named Alan Hildebrand (1955–) wrote about some impact related deposits around the Caribbean that had an age coincident with the Cretaceous-Tertiary boundary. These deposits include brown clay with an anomalous concentration of the metal iridium, thought to be from a meteorite, and some impact melts in the forms of small beads that are called tektites. Hildebrand also wrote about evidence for a giant tsunami around the Caribbean at the K-T boundary, but did not know the location of the crater. It was not until 1990, when Carlos Byars, a reporter for the Houston Chronicle newspaper, put the observations together and contacted Hildebrand, and led Hildebrand and Penfield to work together on realizing that they had located the crater and

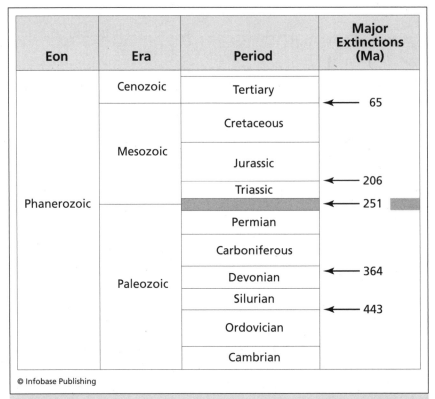

Eon	Era	Period	Major Extinctions (Ma)
Phanerozoic	Cenozoic	Tertiary	←— 65
	Mesozoic	Cretaceous	
		Jurassic	←— 206
		Triassic	←— 251
	Paleozoic	Permian	
		Carboniferous	
		Devonian	←— 364
		Silurian	←— 443
		Ordovician	
		Cambrian	

© Infobase Publishing

Chart showing mass extinctions in geological time. Major extinctions have occurred at the Ordovician-Silurian boundary, near the end of the Devonian, at the Permian-Triassic boundary, and at the Cretaceous-Tertiary boundary. A combination of changing climate, massive global volcanism, and meteorite impacts are thought to be responsible for most mass extinctions.

the deposits of the giant impact from the Cretaceous-Tertiary mass extinction.

Initially, the Chicxulub crater was thought to be about 110 miles (177 km) wide, but later studies have shown that it is a complex crater and an additional ring was located outside the initial discovery, and the crater is now regarded as being 190 miles (300 km) in diameter. The outermost known ring of the Chicxulub crater is marked by a line of sinkholes, where water moved along fractures and dissolved the underlying limestone.

The Chicxulub crater is buried under younger limestone, lying beneath 3,200 feet (1 km) of limestone that overlies 1,600 feet (500 m) of andesitic glass and breccia that are only found within the circular impact structure. These igneous rocks are thought to be impact melts, generated by the melting of the surrounding rocks during the impact

Photo of Permian trilobite fossil Lichas furcifer, County Durham, England *(Photo Researchers)*

event, and the melts rose to fill the crater immediately after the impact. Supporting this interpretation is the presence of some unusual minerals and quartz grains that show evidence for being shocked at high pressures, forming distinctive bands through the mineral grains. The center depression of the crater is about 2,000 to 3,600 feet deep compared to the same layers outside the crater rim, although the surface expression is now minimal since the crater is buried so deeply by younger rocks. The band of sinkholes that marks the outer rim of the crater suggests that the interior of the crater may have been filled with water after the impact, forming a circular lake.

It is estimated that the size of the meteorite that hit Chixculub was six miles (10 km) in diameter, and released an amount of energy equal to 10^{14} tons of TNT. Recent studies suggest that the type of meteorite that hit Chicxulub was a carbonaceous chondrite, based on the chemistry and large amount of carbonaceous material found in pieces of the meteorite recovered from the impact.

The impact at Chicxulub was devastating for the local and global environment. The impact hit near the break between the continental shelf and the continental slope, so it ejected huge amounts of dust into the atmosphere from the shelf, and caused a huge mass of the continental shelf to collapse into the Gulf of Mexico and Caribbean. This in turn generated one of the largest tsunamis known in the history of the planet. This tsunami was thousands of feet (hundreds of m) tall on the Yucatán Peninsula and was still 165–330 feet (50–100 m) tall as it swept into the present day Texas coastline, reaching far inland.

As the impact excavated the crater at Chicxulub, probably in less than a second, the meteorite was vaporized and ejected huge amounts of dust, steam, and ash into the atmosphere. As this material reentered the atmosphere around the planet it would have been heated to incandescent temperatures, igniting global wildfires and quickly heating surfaces and waters. At the same time, tremendous earthquake waves were generated, estimated to have reached magnitudes of 12 or 13 on the open-ended Richter scale. This is larger than any known earthquake since then, and would have resulted in seismic waves that uplifted and dropped the ground surface by hundreds to a thousand feet (up to 300 m) at a distance of 600 miles (965 km) from the crater.

The impact generated huge amounts of dust and particles that would have been caught in the atmosphere for months after the impact, along with the ash from the global fires. This would block the sunlight resulting in ice condition across the planet. Countering this effect is the production and release of huge amounts of carbon dioxide by the vaporization of carbonate rocks during the impact, which would have helped induce a greenhouse warming of climate that could have lasted

Reconstruction of the famous Middle Cambrian Burgess Shale fauna of British Columbia, Canada. Organisms fossilized in the Burgess Shale are thought to represent a community living in shallow water on the upper edge of a steep escarpment. Chunks of this shallow, muddy substrate slumped off the precipice and plummeted into deep water where the contained organisms were rapidly buried under a rain of sediment. The deep, oxygen-depleted water was free of predators, currents, and microbial activity which may have otherwise destroyed the entombed treasures. Known for its remarkable preservations of soft animal and plant tissues, the Burgess Shale provides a rare glimpse of Earth's Cambrian biota. Prominent in the photo are large tube sponges (*Vauxia densa*), smaller branching tube sponges (*Vauxia gracilenta*), knobby rodlike dasycladacean algae (*Margaretia dorus*), a jellyfishlike holothurian (*Eldonia ludwigi*), mats of filamentous algae (*Marpolia spissa*), and a variety of other smaller arthropods, echinoderms, worms, sponges, and animals of unknown affinity. (*Photo Researchers*)

Opposite: Sketches in detail of the Chicxulub impact: (a) a map showing inferred crater rim locations; (b) cross section of the impact site, showing how impact caused massive collapse of the continental shelf margin, initiating submarine slides and gravity flows that powered tsunamis, while on-land part of crater ejected material into atmosphere.

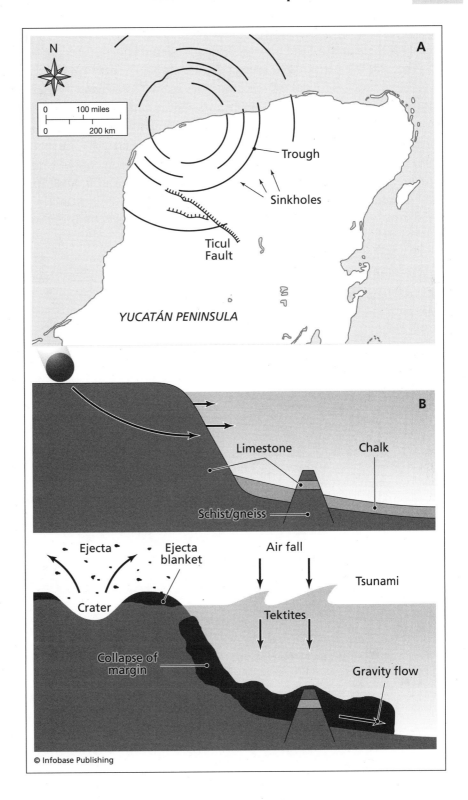

decades. Together, these effects wreaked havoc on the terrestrial fauna and flora that survived the fires and impact related effects.

The Chicxulub crater and impact are widely held to have caused the mass extinction and death of the dinosaurs at the Cretaceous-Tertiary boundary. However, the global environment was considerably stressed before the impact, with marine planktonic organisms seeing a dramatic decline before the impact (and a more dramatic one after the impact), and global temperatures falling before the crash. Some scientists argue that not all fauna, such as frogs, went extinct during the impact and they should have if the impact was the sole cause of mass extinction. Others have argued that the age of the impact is not exactly the same

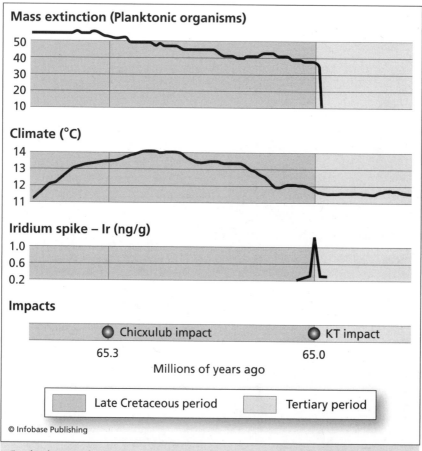

Graphs showing climate change preceding the Chicxulub impact. Temperatures were falling, and many marine planktonic organisms were dying off before the massive impact that triggered the global mass extinction at the Cretaceous-Tertiary boundary.

age as the mass extinction, and may actually predate the extinction by up to 300,000 years. Some models suggest that the global environment was already stressed, and the impact was the final blow to the environment that caused the global mass extinction.

Manicougan Crater, Ontario, Canada

At 62 miles (100 km) across, the Manicougan structure in Ontario is one of the largest known impact structures in Canada, and the fifth largest known impact structure on Earth. This circular, partly exposed crater formed by the impact of a meteorite with a three-mile (5-km) diameter with Earth 214 million years ago, hitting what is now the Precambrian shield. The Manicougan River flows south out of the south side of the crater, and drains into the St. Lawrence River. For some time it was thought that the Manicougan impact was the crater resulting from the impact that caused a mass extinction that killed 60 percent of all species on Earth at the Permian-Triassic boundary, but dating of the impact melt showed that the crater was 12 million years too old to be associated with that event.

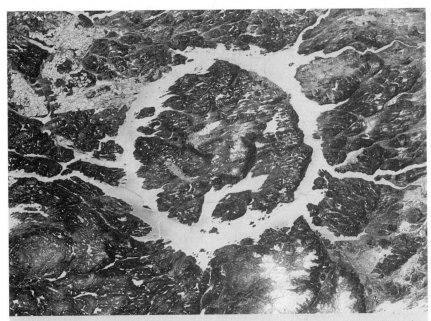

Image of Manicougan crater, Ontario, frozen over in winter: the crater is 43 miles (70 km) in diameter and formed by a meteorite impact 200 million years ago. The crater is now deeply eroded, and filled with water as a hydroelectric reservoir. *(NASA)*

The Manicougan crater has been deeply eroded by the Pleistocene glaciers that scraped the loose sediments off the Canadian shield, pushing them south into the United States. The crater is exposed in bedrock and is currently delineated by two semi-circular lakes that are part of a hydroelectric dam project.

The Manicougan structure has a large central dome, rising 1,640 feet (500 m) above the surrounding surface, culminating at a peak called Mount de Babel. It is also characterized by huge amounts of broken and brecciated rocks, and shatter cones that point in toward the center of the dome. Shatter cones are cone-shaped fractures that form during impacts, from the shock wave of the impact passing through the adjacent rock. Shatter cones usually have points or apexes that point toward the point of impact, but may have more complex patterns that form by the shock waves bouncing off other surfaces in the bedrock.

The Manicougan crater also has a very thick layer of an igneous rock called an impact melt, generated when the force of the impact causes the meteorite and the rock it crashes into to vaporize and melt, and then the melt can fill the resulting crater. The impact melt layer at Manicougan is more than 325 feet (100 m) thick. There have also been some high-pressure mineral phases discovered in the rocks from the Manicougan structure, that form at pressures that could only be formed by meteorite impact, and are impossible to reach by other mechanisms at shallow levels of Earth's crust.

Vredefort Impact Structure, South Africa

The Vredefort dome of South Africa is one of the world's largest and oldest known, well-preserved impact structures. It is located in the late *Archean* Witwatersrand basin, and is a large, multi-ring structure with a diameter of 87 miles (140 km) formed by the impact of a meteorite 1.97 billion years ago.

The geology and structure of the Vredefort dome is complex, and its origin was the subject of debates for many years. As the accompanying map and satellite image show, the crater is characterized by a series of concentric rims of rock outcroppings of

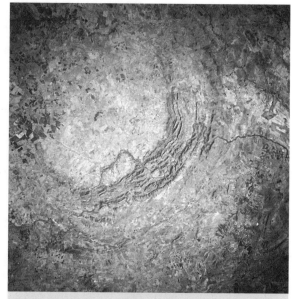

Satellite view of Vredefort Dome in South Africa showing the multiple rings along the rim on the northwest side of the ancient crater (north is to the lower right corner of image) *(NASA)*

the different Precambrian rocks in the area, including the *Protero-zoic* Transvaal Supergroup, and the Archean Ventersdorp and Witwatersrand Supergroups, and the underlying Dominion volcanics and Archean granitic basement. Prior to the impact these rocks formed a shallowly dipping sequence on top of the Archean granitic basement, but the impact was so strong that it excavated a crater then the rocks rebounded, with the Archean basement being uplifted in a steep dome

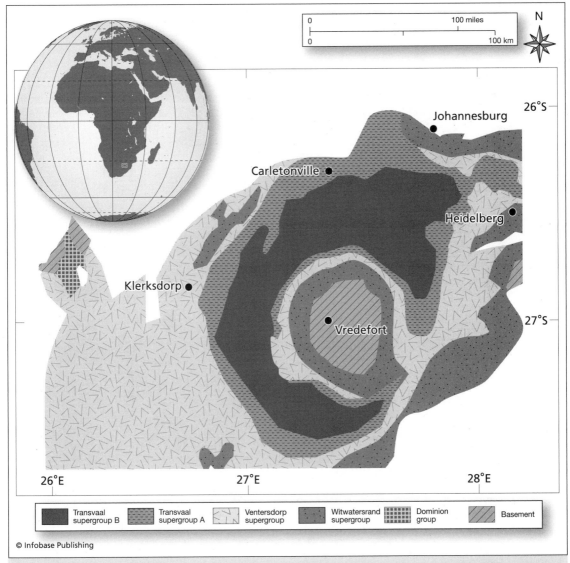

Map of Vredefort Impact Crater, South Africa, with a diameter of 186 miles (300 km). It is thought that this dome formed by the impact of a meteorite with a 6-mile (10-km) diameter striking Earth in South Africa 2.023 billion years ago.

Apex

Fringe

Shatter cone

© Infobase Publishing

The Vredefort Dome was designated an impact crater, owing to shatter cones, which form from the movement of shock waves through rock, from the cone's apex to the fringes. Sketch shows a typical shatter cone from Vredefort

in the central uplift of the crater that rose all the way to the present surface, tilting and folding the surrounding rocks in the process.

The Vredefort dome is famous for hosting a number of geologic features that are diagnostic of meteorite impacts. First, the crater is surrounded by numerous shock metamorphic features, including many impact breccias, some of which are invaded by impact melt glasses called *pseudotachylites.* Many shatter cones have been identified at Vredefort, and the vast majority of these point inward to a point located just above the present day surface, presumably pointing to the place of the initial shock and point of impact. Finally, the Vredefort dome is associated with a number of high-pressure mineral phases including coesite, stishovite, and diaplectic silica glass. These features require pressures of about 25, 75–100, and 120 kilobars (equivalent to depths of up 215 miles or 350 km depth in Earth) to form. Since the surrounding rocks did not reach these pressures, the only known way to form these mineral phases is through meteorite impact.

Lunar Impact Craters

Earth's moon is the closest celestial object, and is covered by many impact craters, large and small. The lack of water, crustal recycling through plate tectonics, and weathering like on Earth has resulted in the preservation of craters that are billions of years old, and provides scientists with a natural laboratory to observe and model impact craters of different sizes and styles. Thousands upon thousands of photographs have revealed the great diversity in styles of lunar craters, and has yielded insight into the cratering mechanisms responsible for cratering events on Earth. The large number of impact craters on the moon also hints at the importance of impact cratering on the early Earth. The moon has a much lower gravity field than Earth, so Earth has a greater chance of attracting and being hit by any nearby asteroids than the moon. Since there are so many impact craters on the Moon, there should have been even more on the early Earth. Crustal recycling, erosion, and weathering have simply erased the surface traces of these impacts. However, their effects, in terms of adding energy, elements, including organic and volatile molecules to Earth is cumulative, and impacts have played a large role in the evolution of the planet.

This is a detailed view of the backside of Moon in the vicinity of Crater No. 308 taken during the *Apollo 11* mission *(NASA)*

NASA missions have also landed on and explored the lunar surface, aiding the understanding of the evolution of Earth-Moon system, including the materials associated with impact events on the moon. *Apollo 11*, the first manned lunar mission, launched from The Kennedy Space Center, Florida, via a *Saturn V* launch vehicle on July 16, 1969, and safely returned to Earth on July 24, 1969. The three-man crew aboard the flight consisted of Neil A. Armstrong, commander; Michael Collins, Command Module pilot; and Edwin E. (Buzz) Aldrin, Jr., Lunar Module pilot. The Lunar Module (LM), named *Eagle*, carrying astronauts Neil Armstrong and Edwin Aldrin, was the first crewed vehicle to land on the Moon. Meanwhile, astronaut Collins piloted the Command Module in a parking orbit around the Moon. Armstrong was the first human to ever stand on the lunar surface, followed by Aldrin. The crew collected 47 pounds of lunar surface material that was returned to Earth for analysis. The surface exploration was concluded in 2.5 hours. With the success of *Apollo 11*, the national objective to land men on the Moon and return them safely to Earth had been accomplished. The samples collected were distributed to research groups around the country, greatly advancing the understanding of formation and evolution of the Moon.

Conclusion

Hundreds of meteorite craters have been identified on Earth. Small craters typically have overturned and uplifted rims, and a semi-circular depression or crater marking the site of the impact. Larger impact craters collapse inward to fill the crater excavated by the impact, and develop a characteristic medial high, and many rims of uplifted and depressed crustal rocks. Impacts are commonly identified on the basis of impact breccias and shatter cones, by impact melts, and by high-pressure mineral phases such as coesite, stishovite, and diplectic glass. Impact craters of all sizes and shapes have been identified on Earth, and the Moon.

Several air bursts from explosions of meteorites above Earth's surface have been witnessed by people in the past century. The largest of these was the explosion above Tunguska, Russia, of a comet or meteorite that caused an explosion that leveled thousands of square miles (km) of trees, and sent atmospheric shock waves around the world. Heat from the explosion sent flash fires across the impact area. The Tunguska area was sparsely populated at the time, but if the meteorite had entered Earth's atmosphere 4 hours and 47 minutes later, it would have exploded above the city of St. Petersburg, destroying that city.

The most famous and perhaps most consequential impact crater is the one at Chicxulub, on the Yucatán Peninsula of Mexico. Here, a six-mile- (10-km-) wide meteorite hit Earth 66 million years ago, generating global fires, giant tsunamis, and ejecting tremendous amounts of dust and carbon dioxide into the atmosphere. The result was a mass extinction event at the Cretaceous-Tertiary boundary, and the loss of many species including the dinosaurs.

4

Mass Extinctions and Catastrophes

Earth has experienced several major impact events that pale all other catastrophes, whether earthquake, volcanic eruption, flood, drought, hurricane, landslide, or tsunami, in comparison. Impacts of Earth with large extraterrestrial objects have been linked to mass extinctions, and potentially could wipe out the human race if a collision of a large meteorite happens with Earth. In this chapter, mass extinctions and their possible relationships to meteorite impacts are examined in more detail, since they represent the largest and most significant natural disasters in the history of Earth. Understanding mass extinctions may someday save the human race from the same fate.

Geologists and paleontologists study the history of life on Earth though detailed examination of that record as preserved in sedimentary rock layers laid down one upon the other. For hundreds of years paleontologists have recognized that many organisms are found in a series of layers, and then suddenly disappear at a certain horizon never to reappear in the succeeding progressively younger layers. These disappearances have been interpreted to mark extinctions of the organisms from the biosphere. After hundreds of years of work, many of these rock layers have been dated by using radioactive decay dating techniques on volcanic rocks in the sequences, and many of these sedimentary rock sequences have been correlated with each other on a global scale. Some

Opposite: Diagram of causes for mass extinctions: (a) shows global climate change such as greenhouse warming, (b) shows massive volcanism, and (c) shows meteorite impact

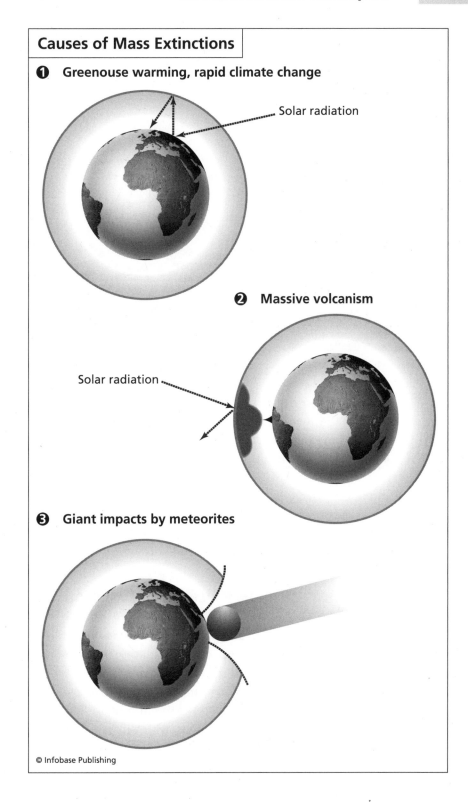

Causes of Mass Extinctions

❶ Greenouse warming, rapid climate change

Solar radiation

❷ Massive volcanism

Solar radiation

❸ Giant impacts by meteorites

Lonar meteorite crater in basalt of the Deccan plateau, Maharashtra, India *(Alamy)*

are associated with other deposits along the layers, indicating unusual concentrations of the metal iridium, carbon from massive fires, and other impact related features such as tektites and tsunami deposits.

One of the more important results that have come from such detailed studies is that the rock record preserves a record of several extinction events that have occurred simultaneously on a global scale. Furthermore, these events do not just affect thousands or hundreds of thousands of members of a species, but they have wiped out many species and families each containing millions or billions of individuals.

The Role of Noncatastrophic Processes in Evolution and Extinction

The progression of life, evolution, and extinction can be influenced or driven by many things other than impacts with space objects such as meteorites and comets. Variations in the style of plate tectonics or the positions of the continents, the supercontinent cycle, and continental collisions can all affect life, evolution, and extinction. Plate tectonics also may cause glaciation and climate changes, which in turn influence evolution and extinction.

One of the primary ways that normal, noncatastrophic plate tectonic mechanisms drive evolution and extinction is through tectonic induced changes to sea level. Fluctuating sea levels cause the global climate to fluctuate between warm periods when shallow seas are easily heated, and cold periods when glaciation draws the water down to place shorelines along the steep continental slopes. Many species cannot tolerate such variations in temperature and drastic changes to their shallow shelf environments, and thus become extinct. After organisms from a specific environment die off, their environmental niches are available for other species to inhabit.

Sea levels have risen and fallen dramatically in Earth history, with water covering all but 5 percent of the land surface at times, and water falling so that continents occupy 40 percent more of the planet's surface at other times. The most important plate tectonic mechanism of changing sea level is to change the average depth of the seafloor by changing the volume of the mid-ocean ridge system. If the undersea ridges take up more space in the ocean basins, then the water will be displaced higher onto the land; much like dropping pebbles into a birdbath may cause it to overflow.

The volume of the *mid-ocean ridge system* can be changed through several mechanisms, all of which have the same effect. Young oceanic crust is hotter, more buoyant, and topographically higher than older crust. Thus, if the average age of the oceanic crust is decreased then more of the crust will be at shallow depths, displacing more water onto the continents. If *seafloor spreading* rates are increased then the average age of oceanic crust will be decreased, the volume of the ridges will be increased, the average age of the seafloor will be decreased, and sea levels will rise. This has happened at several times in Earth history, including during the mid Cretaceous between 110–85 Ma when sea levels were 660 feet (200 m) higher than they are today, covering much of the central United States and other low-lying continents with water. This also warmed global climates, because the sun easily warmed the abundant shallow seas. It has also been suggested that sea levels were consistently much higher in the Precambrian, when seafloor spreading rates were likely to have been generally faster.

Sea levels can also rise from additional magmatism on the seafloor. If Earth goes through a period where seafloor volcanoes erupt more magma on the seafloor, then the space occupied by these volcanic deposits will be displaced onto the continents. The additional volcanic rocks may be erupted at *hot spot* volcanoes like Hawaii, or along the mid-ocean ridge system, either way the result is the same.

A third way for the mid-ocean ridge volume to increase sea level height is to simply have more ridges on the seafloor. At the present time the mid-ocean ridge system is 40,000 miles (65,000 km) long. If Earth goes through a period where it needs to lose more heat, such as in the Precambrian, one of the ways it may do this is by increasing the length of the ridge system where magmas erupt and loose heat to the seawater. Ridge lengths were probably greater in the Precambrian, which together with faster seafloor spreading and increased magmatism may have kept sea levels at high levels for millions of years.

Sea level may also be changed by glaciation, which may be induced by tectonic or astronomical causes. At present glaciers cover much of Antarctica, Greenland, and mountain ranges in several regions. There is approximately 6 million cubic miles (25,000,000 km^2) of ice locked up in glaciers. If this ice were to all melt, then sea levels would rise by 230 feet (70 m) covering many coastal regions, cities, and interior farmland with shallow seas. During the last glacial maximum in the Pleistocene ice ages (20,000 years ago) sea levels were 460 feet (140 m) lower than today, with shorelines up to hundreds of miles (km) seaward of their present locations, along the continental slopes.

Continental collisions and especially the formation of supercontinents can cause glaciations. When continents collide, many of the carbonate rocks deposited on continental shelves are exposed to weathering. As the carbonates and other minerals weather, their weathering products react with atmospheric elements and tend to combine with atmospheric CO_2. Carbon dioxide is a greenhouse gas that keeps the climate warm, and steady reductions of CO_2 in the atmosphere by weathering or other processes lowers global temperatures. Thus, times of continental collision and supercontinent formation tend to be times that draw CO_2 out of the atmosphere, plunging Earth into a cold "icehouse" period. In the cases of supercontinent formation, this icehouse may remain in effect until the supercontinent breaks up, and massive amounts of seafloor volcanism associated with new rifts and ridges add new CO_2 back into the atmosphere.

The formation and dispersal of supercontinent fragments, and migrating land masses in general, also strongly influence evolution and extinction. When supercontinents break up, a large amount of shallow continental shelf area is created. Life-forms tend to flourish in the diverse environments on the continental shelves, and many spurts in evolution have occurred in the shallow shelf areas. In contrast, when continental areas are isolated, such as Australia and Madagascar today, life-forms evolve independently on these continents. If plate tectonics brings these isolated continents into contact, the different species will compete for similar food and environments, and typically only the strongest survive.

The position of continents relative to the spin axes (or poles) of Earth can also influence climate, evolution, and extinction. At times (like the present) when a continent is sitting on one or both of the poles, these continents tend to accumulate snow and ice, and to become heavily glaciated. This causes ocean currents to become colder, lowers global sea levels, and reflects more of the sun's radiation back to space. Together, these effects can put a large amount of stress on species, inducing or aiding extinction.

The History of Life and Mass Extinctions

Life on Earth has evolved from simple organisms known as *Archaea* that appeared on Earth by 3.85 billion years ago. Life may have been here earlier, but the record is not preserved, and the method by which life first appeared is also unknown and the subject of much thought and research by scientists, philosophers, and religious scholars.

The Archaea derive energy from breaking down chemical bonds of carbon dioxide, water and nitrogen, and have survived to this day in environments where they are not poisoned by oxygen. They presently live around hot vents around mid-ocean spreading centers, deep in the ground in pore spaces between soil and mineral grains, and in hot springs. The Archaea represent one of the three main branches of life, the other two branches including the bacteria, and the eukarya. The plant and animal kingdoms are part of the eukarya.

Prokaryotic bacteria (single celled organisms lacking a cell nucleus) were involved in *photosynthesis* by 3.5 billion years ago, gradually transforming atmospheric carbon dioxide to oxygen and setting the stage for the evolution of simple *eukaryotes* in the Proterozoic (containing a cell nucleus and membrane bound organelles). Two and half billion years later, by one billion years ago, cells began reproducing sexually. This long awaited step allowed cells to exchange and share genetic material, speeding up evolutionary changes by orders of magnitude. Oxygen continued to build in the atmosphere, and some of this oxygen was combined into O_3 to make ozone. Ozone forms a layer in the atmosphere that blocks ultraviolet rays of the sun, forming an effective shield against

Ediacarian fauna polychaete worm (*Dickinsonia costata*); Precambrian era, 600 million years old, Ediacara, Australia *(VU)*

this harmful radiation. When the ozone shield became thick enough to block a large portion of the ultraviolet radiation, life began to migrate out of the deep parts of the ocean and deep in land soils, into shallow water and places exposed to the sun. Multicellular life evolved around 670 million years ago, around the same time that the supercontinent of *Gondwana* was forming near the equator. Most of the planet's land masses were joined together for a short while, and then began splitting up and drifting apart again by 550 million years ago. This break up of the supercontinent of Gondwana is associated with the most remarkably diversification of life in the history of the planet. In a remarkably short period of no longer than 40 million years, life developed complex forms with hard shells, and an incredible number of species appeared for the first time. This period of change marked the transition from the Precambrian Era to the Cambrian Period marking the beginning of the Paleozoic Era. The remarkable development of life in this period is known as the Cambrian explosion. In the past 540 million years since the Cambrian explosion, life has continued to diversify with many new species appearing.

The evolution of life-forms is also punctuated with the disappearance or extinction of many species, some as isolated cases, and others that die off at the same time as many other species in the rock record. There are a number of distinct horizons representing times

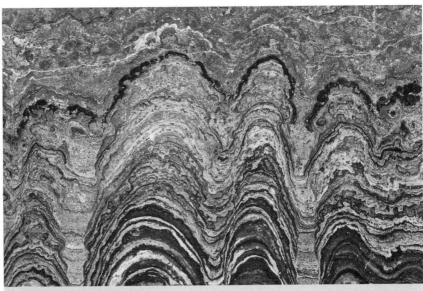
Stromatolite from the Precambrian *(Science Photo Library)*

when hundreds, thousands and even more species suddenly died, being abundant in the record immediately before the formation of one rock layer, and absent immediately above that layer, forever. Mass extinctions are typically followed, after several million years, by the appearance of many new species and the expansion and evolution of old species that did not go extinct. These rapid changes are probably a response to availability of environmental niches vacated by the extinct organisms. The new species rapidly populate these available spaces.

Mass extinction events are thought to represent major environmental catastrophes on a global scale. In some cases these mass extinction events can be tied to specific likely causes, such as meteorite impact or massive volcanism, but in others their cause is unknown. Understanding the triggers of mass extinctions has important and obvious implications for ensuring the survival of the human race.

Examples of Mass Extinctions

Most species are present on Earth for about four million years. Many species come and go during background level extinctions and evolution of new species from old, but the majority of changes occur during the distinct mass dyings and repopulation of the environment. Earth's biosphere has experienced five major and numerous less significant mass extinctions in the past 500 million years (in the Phanerozoic Era). These events occurred at the end of the Ordovician, in the Late Devonian, at the Permian-Triassic boundary, the Triassic-Jurassic boundary, and at the Cretaceous-Tertiary (K-T) boundary.

The early Paleozoic saw many new life-forms emerge in new environments for the first time. The Cambrian explosion led to the development of trilobites, *brachiopods, conodonts*, mollusks, echinoderms, and *ostracods*. Bryozoans, crinoids, and rugose corals joined the biosphere in the Ordovician, and reef-building stromatoporoids flourished in shallow seas. The end-Ordovician extinction is one of the greatest of all Phanerozoic time. About half of all species of brachiopods and bryozoans died off, and more than 100 other families of marine organisms disappeared forever.

The cause of the mass extinction at the end of the Ordovician appears to have been largely tectonic, as no meteorite impacts or massive volcanic outpourings are known from this time. The major landmass of Gondwana had been resting in equatorial regions for much of the Middle Ordovician, but migrated toward the South Pole at the end of the Ordovician. This caused global cooling

Cambrian brachiopod from the Burgess shale *(Photo Researchers)*

and glaciation, lowering sea levels from the high stand they had been resting at for most of the Cambrian and Ordovician. The combination of cold climates with lower sea levels, leading to a loss of shallow shelf environments for habitation, probably were enough to cause the mass extinction at the end of the Ordovician.

The largest mass extinction in Earth history occurred at the Permian-Triassic boundary, over a period of about 5 million years. The Permian world included abundant corals, crinoids, bryozoans, and bivalves in the oceans, and on land, amphibians wandered about amid lush plant life. Ninety percent of oceanic species were to become extinct, and 70 percent of land vertebrates died off at the end of the Permian. This greatest catastrophe of Earth history did not have a single cause, but reflects the combination of various elements.

Ordovician graptolite (*Didymograptus Murchisoni*) from Wales, United Kingdom *(Alamy)*

Coelacanth armored fish, photographed off the Comoros Islands near Madagascar *(Photo Researchers)*

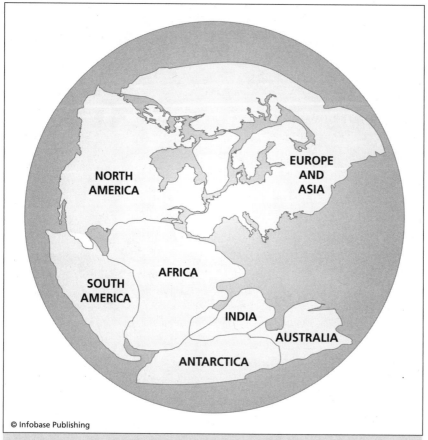

Diagram of the supercontinent of Pangaea as it existed in the late Paleozoic

First, plate tectonics was again bringing many of the planet's land masses together in a supercontinent (this time, Pangaea), causing greater competition for fewer environmental niches by Permian life-forms. Drastically reduced were the rich continental shelf areas. As the continents collided mountains were pushed up, reducing the effective volume of the continents available to displace the sea, so sea levels fell, putting additional stress on life by further limiting the availability of favorable environmental niches. The global climate became dry and dusty, and the supercontinent formation led to widespread glaciation. This lowered sea level even more, lowered global temperatures, and put many life-forms on the planet in a very uncomfortable position. Many perished.

In the final million years of the Permian, the Northern Siberian plains let loose a final devastating blow. The Siberian flood basalts began erupting at 250 million years ago, becoming the largest known

Tyrannosaurus Rex model, Jurassic *(Shutterstock)*

outpouring of continental flood basalts ever. Carbon dioxide was released in hitherto unknown abundance, warming the atmosphere and melting the glaciers. Other gases were also released perhaps also including methane, as the basalts probably melted permafrost and vaporized thick accumulations of organic matter that accumulate in high latitudes like that at which Siberia was located 250 million years ago.

The global biosphere collapsed, and evidence suggests that the final collapse happened in less than 200,000 years, and perhaps in less than 30,000 years. Entirely internal processes may have caused the end-Permian extinction, although some scientists now argue that an impact may have dealt the final death blow. For some time it was argued that the Manicougan impact crater in Canada may be the crater from an impact that caused the Permian-Triassic extinction, but radiometric dating of the Manicougan structure showed it to be millions of years too old to be related to the mass extinction. After the Permian-Triassic extinction was over, new life-forms populated the seas and land, and these Mesozoic organisms tended to be more mobile and adept than their Paleozoic counterparts. The great Permian extinction created opportunities for new life-forms to occupy now empty niches, and the most adaptable and efficient organisms took control. The toughest of the marine organisms survived, and a new class of land animals grew to new proportions and occupied the land and skies. The Mesozoic, time of the great dinosaurs, had begun.

The Triassic-Jurassic extinction is not as significant as the Permian-Triassic extinction. Mollusks were abundant in the Triassic shallow marine realm, with fewer brachiopods, and ammonoids recovered from near total extinction at the Permian-Triassic boundary. Sea urchins became abundant, and new groups of hexacorals replaced the rugose corals. Many land plants survived the end-Permian extinction, including the ferns and seed ferns that became abundant in the Jurassic. Small mammals that survived the end-Permian extinction rediversified in the Triassic, many to only become extinct at the close of the Triassic. Dinosaurs evolved quickly in the late Triassic, starting off small, and attaining sizes approaching 20 feet (6 m) by the end of the Triassic. The giant pterosaurs were the first known flying vertebrate, appearing late in the Triassic. Crocodiles, frogs, and turtles lived along with the dinosaurs. The end of the Triassic is marked by a major extinction in the

Late Jurassic Pterodactylus fossil about the size of a robin *(Photo Researchers)*

marine realm, including total extinction of the conodonts, and a mass extinction of the mammal-like reptiles known as therapsids, and the placodont marine reptiles. Although the causes of this major extinction event are poorly understood, the timing is coincident with the breakup of Pangaea and the formation of major evaporite and salt deposits. It is likely that this was a tectonic-induced extinction, with supercontinent breakup initiating new oceanic circulation patterns, and new temperature and salinity distributions.

After the Triassic-Jurassic extinction, dinosaurs became extremely diverse and many quite large. Birds first appeared at the end of the Jurassic. The Jurassic was the time of the giant dinosaurs, which experienced a partial extinction affecting the largest varieties of Stegosauroids, Sauropods, and the marine Ichthyosaurs and Plesiosaurs. This major extinction is also poorly explained but may be related to global cooling. The other abundant varieties of dinosaurs continued to thrive through the Cretaceous.

The Cretaceous-Tertiary (K-T) extinction is perhaps the most famous of mass extinctions because the dinosaurs perished during this event. The Cretaceous land surface of North America was occupied by bountiful species, including herds of dinosaurs both large and small, some herbivores and other carnivores. Other vertebrates included crocodiles, turtles, frogs, and several types of small mammals. The sky had flying dinosaurs including the vulturelike pterosaurs, and insects including giant dragonflies. The dinosaurs had dense vegetation to feed on, including the flowing angiosperm trees, tall grasses, and many other types of trees and flowers. Life in the ocean had evolved to include abundant bivalves including clams and oysters, ammonoids, and corals that built large reef complexes.

Near the end of the Cretaceous, though the dinosaurs and other life-forms didn't know it, things were about to change. High sea levels produced by mid-Cretaceous rapid seafloor spreading were falling,

POPULATION GROWTH AND THE FUTURE

Humans are experiencing a population explosion that cannot be sustained by the planet's limited resources. At some point, fresh water and food sources will not be able to sustain the global population, and hunger, famine, disease, and war will follow. Natural disasters will be more disastrous because the environmental stresses on the global population will already be high. People are migrating in huge numbers to hazard-prone areas including coastlines, river flood plains, and the flanks of active volcanoes. Natural geologic hazards in these areas will cause disasters, and thousands of people will be affected. Perhaps greater understanding of natural geologic hazards will cause people to move to safer areas, or to be better prepared for the hazards in the areas in which they live.

The population of the human race has exploded so dramatically for a number of reasons. About a million years ago there are estimated to have been a few thousand migratory humans on Earth, and by about ten thousand years ago this number had increased to only 5–10 million. It wasn't until about eight thousand years ago when humans began stable agricultural practices and domesticated some species of animals that the population rate started to increase substantially. The increased standards of living and nutrition caused the population growth to soar to about 200 million by 2,000 years ago, and 100 million by 1,000 years ago. By the 18th century, humans began manipulating their environments more, began public health services, and began to recognize and seek treatments for diseases that were previously taking many lives. The average life span began to soar, and world population surpassed 1 billion in the year 1810. A mere 100 years later, world population doubled again to 2 billion, and had reached 4 billion by 1974. World population is now close to 7 billion and climbing more rapidly than at any time in history, doubling every 50 years. This rate of growth is not sustainable—at this rate, in about 800 years, there will be one human for every three square feet (3 feet by 1 foot) (0.27 m^2) on Earth.

It is not clear what humans will do when the population exceeds the ability of Earth to support this increased population. History shows that population stress often leads nations and ethnic groups

(continues)

(continued)

to conflict and war, whereas in other cases isolated societies such as the Anasazi of the American southwest reached their capacity to be supported by the land's natural resources and vanished. With these history lessons, it is necessary to consider, and plan for ways to reduce the possibility that humans could succumb to disease and famine, perhaps induced by drought. It is also necessary to consider whether a huge natural disaster such as an impact from outer space might send global populations back to a small fraction of the current level. Nations need to consider ways to deflect Earth-bound asteroids, or prepare to leave.

Cultural changes could decrease the population growth rate, or even the global population. Some evidence suggests that the population growth rate is decreasing in developed countries, and continues to rise in undeveloped and third-world countries. This could be in response to increased medical care reducing the need to have many children to ensure that some survive to adulthood, or it could be a reflection of increased opportunities for women in developed societies.

Humans are causing mass extinction on a global scale that rivals the mass extinctions caused by massive flood basalt volcanism and meteorite impacts. Thousands of species are vanishing every year. Familiar to many is the rapid global decline in amphibians, particularly the frogs, in the past few decades. The decline of amphibians could be a sign of global changes and climate changes, or could be from some other factor such as disease. People are destroying environments and through uncontrolled population growth and are competing for limited resources, causing a rapid decrease in global diversity. Humans are destroying many of the organisms that may be crucial to the race's survival, perhaps without even knowing it. Interrelationships between different organisms are complex. The human race may find itself at the point of someday realizing that simple bacteria that went extinct, or the fungi that disappeared a few years back, were essential for some process needed to survive, such as removing some greenhouse gas from the atmosphere. Rarely does one change in the environment go without consequence. Death of one species may allow another to expand, and this new species may be a predator to a third, or carry parasites that can wipe out large segments of the population. Exponential population growth is hazardous, and could be a self-regulating phenomena, with growth leading to greater hazards that will reduce the population in major disasters.

decreasing environmental diversity, cooling global climates, and creating environmental stress. Massive volcanic outpourings in the Deccan Traps and the Seychelles formed as the Indian Ocean rifted apart and magma rose from an underlying mantle plume. Massive amounts of greenhouse gases were released, raising temperatures and stressing the environment. Many marine species were going extinct, and others became severely stressed. Then one bright day a visitor from space about six miles across slammed into the Yucatán Peninsula of Mexico, instantly forming a fireball 1,200 miles (2,000 km) across, followed by giant tsunamis perhaps thousands of feet (hundreds of m) tall. The dust from the fireball plunged the world into a dusty fiery darkness,

Fossil mammal skeleton Eohippus from Tertiary *(Alamy)*

months or years of freezing temperatures, followed by an intense global warming. Few species handled the environmental stress well, and more than a quarter of all the plant and animal kingdom families including 65 percent of all species on the planet became extinct forever. Dinosaurs, mighty rulers of the Triassic, Jurassic, and Cretaceous, were gone forever. Oceanic reptiles and ammonoids died off, and 60 percent of marine planktonic organisms went extinct. The great K-T extinctions affected not only the numbers of species, but also the living biomass—the death of so many marine plankton alone amounted to 40 percent of all living matter on Earth at the time. Similar punches to land-based organisms decreased the overall living biomass on the planet to a small fraction of what it was before the K-T knockout blow.

Some evidence suggests that the planet is undergoing the first stages of a new mass extinction. In the past one hundred thousand years, the ice ages have led to glacial advances and retreats, sea-level rises and falls, the appearance and rapid explosion of human (*Homo sapiens sapiens*) populations, and the mass extinction of many large mammals. In Australia 86 percent of large (> 100 pounds) animals have become extinct in the past 100,000 years, and in South America, North America, and Africa the extinction is an alarming 79 percent, 73 percent, and 14 percent. This ongoing mass extinction appears to be the result of cold climates and more importantly, predation and environmental destruction by

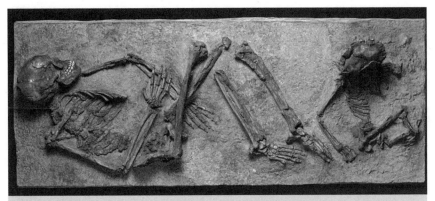

Qafzeh human remains. Fossilized human bones from the Qafzeh cave site in Nazareth, Israel. This may be a ritual burial of a mother with her child (right). These bones are thought to be around 90,000–100,000 years old, and are some of the earliest known examples of *Homo sapiens sapiens*, anatomically modern humans. *(Science Photo Library)*

humans. The loss of large bodied species in many cases has immediately followed the arrival of humans in the region, with the clearest examples being found in Australia, Madagascar, and New Zealand. Similar loss of races through disease and famine has accompanied many invasions and explorations of new lands by humans throughout history.

Conclusion

The history of life on Earth shows that many species exist relatively unchanged for long periods of time, and may diversify or become more specialized, in part in response to environmental changes. Occasionally, huge numbers of different species and individuals within species suddenly die off or are killed in mass extinction events. Some of these seem to result from a combination of severe environmental stresses, greatly enhanced volcanism, or a combination of different effects. Most mass extinction events are now known to also be associated with an impact event. However, not all large impact events are associated with a mass extinction, with a prime example being the Manicougan impact structure which formed from an impact 214 million years ago, 12 million years older than the Permian-Triassic mass extinction. It seems that mass extinctions may be triggered by a combination of different forces all acting together, including environmental stresses from changes in climate associated with plate tectonics and orbital variations, from massive volcanism, and from impacts of meteorites or comets with Earth.

5

Hazards of Impacts and Mitigating the Dangers of Future Impacts

The chances of Earth being hit by a meteorite are small at any given time, but they are greater than the chances of winning a lottery. The chances of dying from an impact are about the same as dying in a plane crash, for a person who takes one flight per year. These comparisons are statistical flukes however, and reflect the fact that a large meteorite impact is likely to kill so many people that it raises the statistical chances of dying by impact. A globally catastrophic impact is generally thought of as one that kills more than 25 percent of the world's population, or currently about 1.6 billion people. Earth has been hit by a number of small impacts, and by some very large impacts that have had profound effects on the life on Earth at those times. It is widely held that an impact caused the extinction of the dinosaurs, and caused many of the other mass extinctions in Earth history, so it is reasonable to assume that a large impact would have serious consequences for life on Earth. Nations of the world need to consider more seriously the threat from meteorite impacts. Impacts that are the size of the blast that hit Siberia at Tunguska in 1908 happen about once every thousand years, and major impacts, that can seriously affect climate and life on Earth, are thought to occur about every 300,000 years. Events like the impact at Chicxulub, that killed the dinosaurs and resulted in a mass extinction, are thought to occur once every 100 million years. The Chicxulub impact initiated devastating global wildfires that consumed much of the biomass on the planet, and sent trillions of tons of submicrometer dust into the stratosphere. After the flash fires, the planet became dark for many months, the atmospheric and ocean chemistry were changed, and the climate experienced a short term but dramatic change. The global ecosystem was practically destroyed, and one of the greatest mass extinctions in geological time resulted. Events that approach or exceed this size place the entire population of the world at risk, and threaten the survival of the human species. Much smaller events have the potential to destroy agricultural produce in fields around the world, leading to an instant global food shortage and mass starvation, collapse of global economies, and political strife.

There are thousands of near-Earth objects that have the potential to hit Earth and form impact craters of various sizes. Most of these objects are asteroids diverted from the main asteroid belt, and long-period comets. A couple of hundred of these objects are in Earth-crossing orbits. There is a wide range in the size, density, size, and composition of these near-Earth objects, all of which can play a role in the type of hazard the body poses as it enters Earth's atmosphere and falls to the surface. In most instances, for objects greater than several hundred feet (~100 m) in diameter, size is the most important factor, and the controlling factor on the style and hazard of the impact is related to the kinetic energy of the object.

This chapter examines the specific hazards associated with large and minor impacts, and then discusses ways that some of these risks may be reduced. Passage of atmospheric shock waves, followed by huge solid Earth quakes, is described, followed by analysis of the tsunamis generated by ocean-hitting impacts. The atmospheric fires associated with the impact, followed by blocking of the Sun by particulate matter thrown up by the impact and fires, is considered to be one of the most hazardous elements of impacts through which many organisms would struggle to survive.

Mitigation strategies for avoiding large impacts of asteroids with Earth involve first locating and tracking objects in Earth crossing orbits. If a collision appears imminent, then efforts should be made to try to deflect the asteroid out of the collision course by blasting it with

Opposite: Graphs showing (a) the frequency/power of impacts with different megatons of TNT equivalency, with some known examples and comparisons, and (b) frequency of impacts of different sizes (NASA)

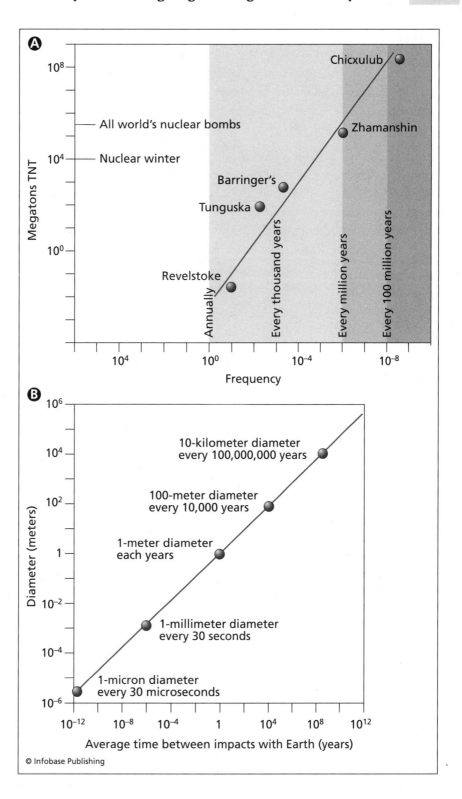

rockets, or mounting rockets on the asteroid to steer it away. Alternatively, if the asteroid is so big, a population from Earth would need to escape the planet to start a new civilization on a new planet. Although seemingly far-fetched, such strategies have been discussed by NASA scientists.

Atmospheric Shock Waves

The effect that an asteroid or meteorite has on Earth's atmosphere depends almost completely on the size of the object. Weak meteorites that are up to about 30–90 feet (10–30 m) in diameter usually break up into fragments and completely burn up in the atmosphere before they hit Earth's surface. The height in the atmosphere that these meteorites break up depends on the strength of the meteorite body, with most comets and carbonaceous chondrites of this size breaking up above 19 miles (30 km). Stronger meteorites, such as irons, in this size range may make it to the surface.

Meteorites and comets that enter Earth's atmosphere typically are traveling with a velocity of about 6 miles/second (10 km/sec), or 21,600 miles per hour (37,754 km/hr). Small meteorites enter the upper atmosphere every day, and more rarely, large ones enter, and compress and heat the air in front of them as they race toward the surface. This heat causes most of these bodies to burn up or explode before they reach the surface, with blasts the size of the Hiroshima or Nagasaki atomic bombs happening daily somewhere in the upper atmosphere, by meteorites that are about 30 feet (10 m) in diameter. Larger meteorites explode closer to the surface and can generate huge air blasts like the explosion that leveled thousands of square miles (km) or trees in Siberia in 1908.

The flux of meteorites of different sizes is calculated in part by comparing crater density on the Moon with the expected result in the higher gravity field of Earth. Larger bodies that make it though the atmosphere hit with a greater frequency for the small objects, and less often for the larger bodies. Meteorites in the 30 foot (10 m) diameter range release about as much energy as the nuclear bomb that was dropped on Hiroshima (0.01 megaton [9,070 tonnes]) of TNT equivalent) when they enter the atmosphere and burn before hitting the surface. Events of this size happen about one time per year on Earth, whereas larger events in the 1 megaton (1 megaton = 1,000,000 tons) range occur about once a century, associated with the burning up of 100 foot (30 m) diameter bodies as they plunge through the atmosphere.

COLLISION OF COMET SHOEMAKER-LEVY WITH JUPITER

In March 1993, Comet Shoemaker-Levy was discovered and predicted to be on a collision course with Jupiter. The prediction was fulfilled in July 2004, when 20 nuclei of the comet crashed into Jupiter, providing astronomers and other scientists with their first closely observed comet-planet impact event.

Comets have undoubtedly played a large role in bringing much if not most of the carbon, oxygen, and nitrogen to Earth and many other planets, forming the oceans and atmosphere, and providing the building blocks for life. Observations of a comet-planet impact yielded insight into this process, and the impacts of the 20 nuclei were even more spectacular than anticipated by the scientists observing the phenomena.

Comet Shoemaker-Levy was discovered on March 25, 1993, by Gene (1928-97) and Carolyn (1929-) Shoemaker, and David Levy (1948-), working from the Palomar Observatory in San Diego, California. The initial discovery of the comet revealed that it was an elongate or rodlike object near Jupiter, which the team hypothesized might be due to tidal forces from Jupiter breaking up a comet into many pieces, each 1.2–2.5 miles (2–4 km) across, which was later confirmed by observations from Kitt Peak Observatory in Arizona. Soon, as astronomers around the world made many observations and measurements, it became apparent that comet Shoemaker-Levy was on a collision course with Jupiter, and it did not have long to go before impact. The comet had been spiraling toward the giant planet, in the grip of its strong gravity for decades, and was broken apart by gravitational forces during a close encounter with Jupiter in 1992.

The fragments began colliding with Jupiter on July 16 at 20:11, and all the fragments had collided by 8:06 on July 22. Over a period of just five and a half days, at least 20 large cometary fragments hit the planet, each causing independent impact effects. If a similar sequence of 20 impacts hit Earth over such a short period, the sequence would have started as terrifying, moved into catastrophic, and ended with a quiet world, probably devoid of life on the surface.

Jupiter is a very different kind of planet than Earth—its surface is gaseous, a mass of swirling clouds—so impacts on Jupiter are quite different from those on Earth. As the comet fragments approached collision, the distance between the fragments lengthened, and some disappeared from view. The impacts were imaged by numerous telescopes around the world, and by the *Galileo* spacecraft. Each had a spectacular fireball, impact flash, and was followed by large dark clouds that rose from the planet's depths. Over a period of a week, these clouds rose to heights in the atmosphere where there are few winds, so they had to gradually dissipate by gravity over long periods of time, beginning to fade after 10–20 days, and some dark clouds lasting more than a month.

It is generally believed that the impact of a 1.2 mile (2 km) object with Earth happens every half million years, ejecting vast quantities of dust into the atmosphere, with severe implications for global climate and life. The unexpectedly large amounts of dark clouds released during the impact of Shoemaker-Levy with Jupiter in 1994 has led many scientists to believe that smaller impacts may be more significant than thought, and that impacts with severe consequences for life may happen more often than every 500,000 years.

A moderate-sized impact event, such as a collision with a meteorite with a 5–10 mile (8–16 km) diameter, moving at a moderate velocity of 7.5 miles/sec (12 km/sec), would release energy equivalent to 100 megatons, or about 1,000 times the yield of all existing nuclear

Effects of Impacts as a Function of Energy and Crater Size

ENERGY OF IMPACT (MEGATONS)	DIAMETER OF METEORITE OR COMET	CRATER DIAMETER MILES (KM)	CONSEQUENCES
< 10			Detonation of stones and comets in upper atmosphere. Irons penetrate surface.
10^1–10^2	245 feet (75 m)	1 (1.5)	Irons form craters (Meteor Crater). Stones produce airbursts (Tunguska). Land impacts destroy an area the size of a city (Washington, Paris).
10^2–10^3	525 feet (160 m)	1.9 (3)	Irons and stones produce ground-bursts, comets produce air bursts. Land impacts destroy an area the size of a large urban area (New York, Cairo).
10^3–10^4	1,150 feet (350 m)	3.7 (6)	Impacts on land produce craters. Ocean impacts produce significant tsunamis. Land impacts destroy area size of small state (Delaware, Israel).
10^4–10^5	0.43 miles (0.7 km)	7.5 (12)	Tsunamis reach oceanic scales, exceeding damage from land impacts. Land impacts destroy area size of a moderate state (Virginia, Taiwan).
10^5–10^6	1.06 miles (1.7 km)	18.7 (30)	Land impacts raise enough dust to affect climate, and freeze crops. Ocean impacts generate hemispheric tsunamis. Global destruction of ozone. Land impacts destroy area size of large state (California, France).
10^6–10^7	1.9 miles (3 km)	37 (60)	Both land and ocean impacts raise dust, impact ejecta is global, changes global climate. Widespread fires. Land impacts destroy area size of a large nation (Mexico, India).
10^7–10^8	4.3 miles (7 km)	78 (125)	Global conflagration, prolonged climate effects, probably mass extinction. Direct destruction of continental scale area (United States, Australia).
10^8–10^9	10 miles (16 km)	155 (250)	Large mass extinction (K-T in scale).
10^9–10^{10}			Survival of all life threatened.

Note: table based on David Morrison, Clark Chapman, and Paul Slovic (*The Impact Hazard*, 1994).

weapons on Earth. The meteorite would begin to glow brightly as it approached Earth, encountering the outer atmosphere. As this body entered the atmosphere, it would create a huge fireball that crashes with Earth after about ten seconds. Events of this magnitude happen about once every thousand years on Earth, but obviously even in this energy range, impacts are not posing serious threats to the survival of life on Earth.

Objects that break up lower than 12 miles (20 km) above the surface cause much greater destruction. Objects about 165 feet (50 m) in diameter that break up at this height will generate significant airbursts that pose significant hazards. Larger objects will strike the ground, releasing energy in a manner similar to atomic bomb blasts (but without releasing radioactivity), with the amount of energy proportional to the size of the meteorite or comet. The impact that hit Tunguska in 1908 is estimated to have released about 10–20 megatons (.91–18 megatonnes), with a radius of complete destruction of 15 miles (25 km), and a much larger affected area. The area of destruction increases to the ⅔ power of the magnitude of the blast.

Solid Earth Shock Wave and Earthquakes

When meteorites hit the surface of Earth they generate seismic waves, and cause earthquakes. The size of the earthquake is related to the energy released by the impactor, which is related to its mass and its velocity. The larger the energy released on the surface, the larger the earthquake. Meteorites that explode in the atmosphere can also generate earthquakes, as the air blast transfers energy to the surface and also generates seismic waves.

Large impacts generate seismic waves that travel through the interior of Earth and along the surface layers. For comparison, the Tunguska explosion and air burst generated a seismic event with a Richter magnitude that is only estimated to be about a magnitude 5 earthquake. In contrast, the Chicxulub impact at the Cretaceous-Tertiary boundary generated a magnitude 11, 12, or 13 earthquake, shaking the entire planet, and resulting in seismic waves that uplifted and dropped the ground surface by hundreds to a thousand feet (up to 300 m) at a distance of 600 miles (965 km) from the crater.

If an impact of this size and energy hit Earth today, shock waves would be felt globally as earthquakes of unimaginable size, destroying much of the surface of the planet, and killing billions of people.

Tsunamis

If a large meteorite strikes the ocean, huge tsunamis would be formed, hundreds and perhaps thousands of feet tall (hundreds of m). These would run up on coastlines, washing away the debris from the earthquakes of a few moments or hours before. Impacts that hit water cause devastation over a larger area than impacts that hit land because of the far-traveling effects of the tsunamis. Impacts that have an energy release of 1,000 megatons (907 megatonnes) should generate tsunamis about 15 feet (5 m) tall and travel more than 600 miles (1,000 km). For impacts that are significantly larger than this (above 10,000 megatons [9,070 megatonnes]) the damage from the tsunami is much greater, and covers a much larger area than the damage from the blast of the impactor itself. The tsunami associated with the Chicxulub impact on the Yucatán Peninsula may have initially been thousands of feet (hundreds of m) high, washing over much of the Gulf Coast of the United States and Mexico, and devastating the Caribbean.

Global Firestorm and Global Winter

The force of large and medium scale impacts eject enormous quantities of superheated dust and gases into the atmosphere, some of which would fall back to Earth as flaming fireballs. Most of the dust would make it into the upper atmosphere where it would encircle the entire planet. The energy from the impact would heat the atmosphere to such a degree that it would spontaneously ignite forests and much of the biomass, sending dark clouds of smoke into the atmosphere. This smoke and the dust from the impact would block out the Sun, leading to a rapid plunge into a dark mini-ice age with most of the Sun's energy blocked from reaching Earth, preventing photosynthesis and plant growth. This darkness and cold would last for several months as the dust slowly settled, forming a global layer of dust recording the chemical signature of the impact. This chemical signature of impacts includes a hallmark high concentration of the rare element iridium, produced by vaporization of the meteorite.

Gradually, rain would remove the sulfuric acid and dust from the atmosphere, but the chemical consequences include enhanced acid rain, which rapidly dissolves calcium carbonates from limestone and shells, releasing carbon dioxide to the atmosphere. The acid rain wreaks havoc on the ocean biosphere, changing the ocean chemistry to the point at which many life-forms become extinct. The carbon dioxide released to

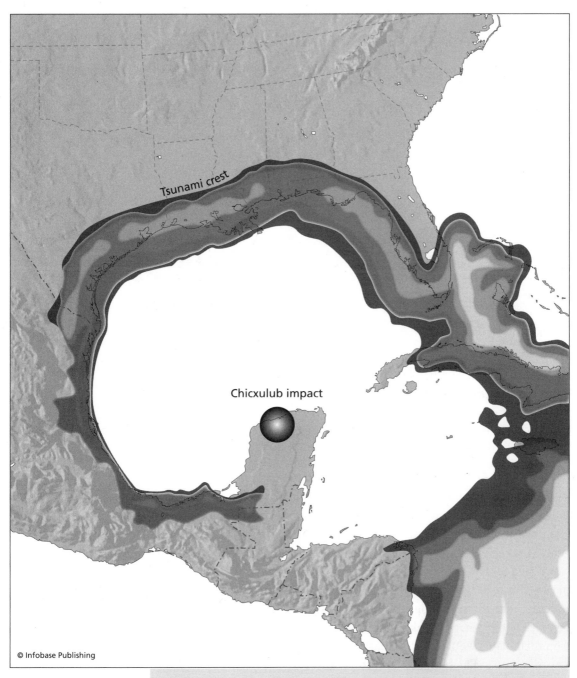

Sketch of model of tsunami four hours after the Chicxulub impact at the Cretaceous-Tertiary boundary. The tsunami generated by this impact may have been several hundred feet (> 100 m) tall when it swept across the Gulf of Mexico shores, through the southern United States, and across the Caribbean.

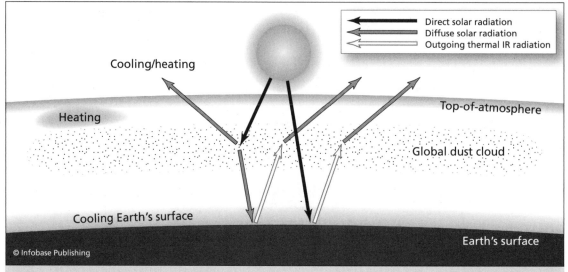

Sketch of atmospheric hazards of impact. After the global firestorms associated with the time immediately after the impact, dust ejected into the atmosphere from the impact and the global fires will act as aerosols, scattering and absorbing incoming solar radiation, cooling the surface of the planet, and warming the upper atmosphere.

the atmosphere heats the planet a few months after the impact, and the planet would enter an extended warm period caused by this greenhouse effect. Temperatures would be more than 10° hotter on average, shifting climate belts and leading to excessively long hot summers.

Mitigating the Dangers of Future Impacts

Collision of a meteorite about a mile (1.6 km) across with Earth would do enough damage to wipe out about a quarter of the human race, and events of this magnitude may occur approximately every three million years. Larger events happen less frequently, and smaller events occur more frequently. It is estimated that about 50 objects with diameters of 50–100 feet (15–30 m) pass between Earth and Moon every day, though these rarely collide with Earth. Comets and stony meteorites of this size will typically break up upon entering the atmosphere, whereas iron meteorites would tend to make it all the way to the planet. Luckily, few of the near-Earth objects are iron meteorites.

To date, there have only been limited efforts by the nations of the world to monitor near-Earth objects and to try to prevent large mete-orites from crashing into Earth and wiping out much of the popula-tion and biosphere. NASA has estimated that there are about 2,000 near-Earth objects greater than half a mile (1 km) in diameter, and that

Photo of the Cretaceous-Tertiary (K-T) boundary layer made of clay containing iridium, between older Cretaceous (K) and younger Tertiary (T) rocks. The boundary is less than an inch (2 cm) thick and here marked by a coin, separating two beds of marine limestone. The K-T layer, a phenomenon worldwide, is thought to be associated with ejected material from the impact of a large extraterrestrial object (comet or meteorite) around 65 million years ago. Photographed near Gubbio, Italy. *(Prof. Walter Alvarez/Photo Researchers)*

about half of them may eventually hit Earth. However, the time interval between individual impacts is greater than 100,000 years. If any of these objects hits Earth, the death toll will be tremendous, particularly if any of them hit populated areas or a major city. Collision of Earth with an asteroid only a mile or two (several km) in diameter would release as much energy as that released by the simultaneous explosion of several million nuclear bombs.

It is now technically feasible to map and track many of the large objects that could be on an Earth-impacting trajectory, and this is being done to some degree. Greater efforts would involve considerable expense to advanced societies, principally the taxpayers of the United States. NASA, working with the United States Air Force, has mounted a preliminary program for mapping and tracking objects in near-Earth orbit, and has already identified many significant objects. Lawmakers and the public must decide if greater expenses are worth the calculated risk of the hazards of impacts hitting Earth. Risk assessment typically involves many variables, such as the likelihood of an event happening,

Artist's rendition of *Hayabusa* (MUSES-C) on Itokawa asteroid 25143 *(JAXA)*

Artist's rendition of *Near Earth Asteroid Rendezvous* (NEAR) spacecraft and EROS asteroid *(Getty)*

how many deaths or injuries would result, and what can be done to reduce the risk. Also, other questions need to be asked such as is it more realistic to try to stop the spread of disease, crime, poverty, famine, and preparing for other natural disasters, or whether resources should be spent looking for objects that might one day collide with Earth. If an asteroid is determined to be on a collision course with Earth, some type of asteroid deflection strategy would need to be employed to attempt to prevent the collision.

Spaceguard is a term that refers to a number of different efforts to search for and monitor near-Earth objects. The United States Congress published a Spaceguard Survey Report, mandating that 90 percent of all large near-Earth objects be located by 2002, and some programs were funded at a level of several million dollars per year toward this goal. Present estimates are that the original goal will be met by the year 2020. One of these efforts is the Catalina Sky Survey, which discovered 310 near-Earth objects in 2005, 400 in 2006, and 450 in 2007. There is a

Artist's rendition of missiles that could be used to blast asteroid out of collision course with Earth *(Photo Researchers)*

loose organization of observers and astronomers in several countries that meet through the International Astronomical Union about asteroid detection. However, it is noteworthy that these efforts were not sufficient to detect two meteorite impacts with Earth including explosion over the Mediterranean in 2002, and the crash of a meteorite in the Bodaybo area of Siberia on September 25, 2002. The meteorites were detected by United States military anti-missile defense satellites only as they entered Earth's atmosphere.

Societies have the technology to attempt to divert or blow up the meteorite using nuclear devises. Bombs could be exploded near the asteroid or meteorite in an attempt to move it out of Earth orbit, or to break it up into small enough pieces that would break up upon entering the atmosphere. Alternatively, given enough time, rockets could be installed on the meteorite and fired to try to steer it out of its impact trajectory. However, many asteroids rotate rapidly, and rockets mounted on these asteroids would not be so effective at changing their course. Other proposals have been made, including firing massive missiles at the asteroid, transferring kinetic energy to move it out of its collision course. However, if the object if very large it is likely that even all of the nuclear weapons or bombs on the planet would not have a significant effect on altering the trajectory of the meteorite or asteroid. Strategies for preventing catastrophic collisions of meteorites with Earth fall into two general categories, including those that attempt to destroy or fragment the asteroid into small pieces that would burn up upon passing though Earth's atmosphere, and strategies that attempt to divert the asteroid, and move it out of its trajectory toward Earth. In some cases it may be enough to simply delay the arrival time of the asteroid with Earth's orbit so that the planet is no longer at the place where it would collide with the asteroid when it crosses Earth's orbit. Such strategies use less energy than blasting the asteroid out of the solar system.

NUCLEAR ATTACK

One of the most popular ideas for deflecting asteroids away from a potential collision with Earth is to fire many nuclear missiles at the asteroid, with the idea that the blast would vaporize the asteroid, eliminating the danger. However, the energy requirements may not be attainable with the world's current arsenal of nuclear weapons, as there are currently no nuclear weapons that release enough energy to destroy an asteroid only a half mile (1 km) in diameter. If enough, or large enough blasts could be directed at an incoming asteroid, it is likely that the blasts would simply fragment the asteroid into many pieces, which would then fall to Earth along with the radiation from the nuclear explosions.

Instead of aiming nuclear blasts directly at any incoming asteroid, it may be possible to divert the orbit of the asteroid by exploding many nuclear bombs near the asteroid, and the energy released from these blasts could effectively steer the asteroid away from its collision course with Earth. Such a strategy has been shown to be theoretically possible by a study called Project Icarus published by a group of researchers from Massachusetts Institute of Technology.

KINETIC IMPACT STRATEGIES

One of the alternative strategies that may be effective in deflecting an asteroid from Earth orbit is to send a massive space craft to collide with the asteroid, altering its momentum and removing it from the collision course. This strategy is currently the object of a major study and mission, called Don Quijote, by the European Space Agency. Early results from this mission have shown that it is possible, and a model of the deflection of near-Earth asteroid 99942 Apophis shows that it would only take a spacecraft with a mass of less than one ton (.9 tonne) to deflect the asteroid out of its modeled collision course with Earth.

GRAVITATIONAL TRACTOR STRATEGIES

Many asteroids and comets are composed of piles of disconnected rubble. Deflection strategies that rely on kinetic impact or deflection by explosion would not necessarily work on these types of asteroids, since any impact would only deflect the fragment that it directly hit. One alternative type of deflection strategy involves slowly moving these asteroid rubble piles by moving a massive spacecraft near the asteroid, and letting the gravitational attraction of the spacecraft slowly pull the asteroid out of threatening orbit. Since both the asteroid and the spacecraft would have a mutual gravitational attraction, the asteroid could be slowly pulled in one direction if small rockets on the spacecraft are used to counter the attraction toward the asteroid, and slowly pull it out of harm's way. This strategy would take several years to be effective.

OTHER STRATEGIES

A number of other strategies have been proposed that could eventually be developed into working deflection missions for asteroids heading toward Earth. One proposal is to focus solar energy at the surface of the asteroid, vaporizing material from the surface, eventually deflecting it from its collision course. It may be possible to wrap incoming asteroids with reflective sheeting, or adding reflective dust to the surface, so that part of the asteroid receives additional radiation from the Sun, and radiation pressure distributed unequally on the asteroid may be enough to deflect it from its orbit. Another idea is to attach a large solar sail to the asteroid, which would absorb solar energy, and change its orbit.

Recent Near Collisions

Collisions between asteroids can alter their orbits and cause them to head into an Earth orbit-crossing path. At this point, the asteroid becomes hazardous to life on Earth, and is known as an Apollo object. It is estimated by NASA and the United States Air Force that there are about 20,000 objects in space that could be on Earth orbit-crossing trajectories. Presently, about 150 Apollo objects with diameters of greater than half a mile (1 km) are known, and a couple of thousand objects this size are known in the entire near-Earth object group. Objects larger than 460 feet (140 m) hit Earth on average about once every 5,000 years. Only in 1996 an asteroid about one quarter mile (half km) across nearly missed hitting Earth, speeding past at a distance about equal to the distance to the Moon. The sobering reality of this near collision is that the asteroid was not even spotted until a few days before it sped past Earth. If the object was bigger, or slightly closer, it might not have been stoppable, and if not, its collision might have had major consequences for life on Earth. A similar near-miss event was recorded again in 2001; Asteroid 2001 YB5, passed Earth at a distance of twice that to the Moon, and it too was not recognized until two weeks before its near-miss. If YB5 hit Earth, it would have released energy equivalent to 350,000 times the energy released during the nuclear bomb blast in Hiroshima.

The objects that are in Earth orbit-crossing paths could not have been in this path for very long, because gravitational influences of Earth, Mars, and Venus would cause them to hit one of the planets or be ejected from the solar system within about 100 million years. The abundance of asteroids in an Earth orbit-crossing path demonstrates that ongoing collisions in the asteroid belt are replenishing the source of potential impacts on Earth. A few rare meteorites found on Earth have chemical signatures that suggest they originated on Mars and on the Moon, probably being ejected toward Earth from giant impacts on those bodies.

Other objects from space may collide with Earth. Comets are masses of ice and carbonaceous material mixed with silicate minerals that are thought to originate in the outer parts of the solar system, in a region called the Oort Cloud. Other comets have a closer origin, in the Kuiper Belt just beyond the orbit of Neptune. There is considerable debate about whether small icy Pluto, considered to be the small outermost planet until recently (see sidebar on page 8), should actually be classified as a large Kuiper Belt object. Comets may be less common near Earth than meteorites, but they still may hit Earth with severe consequences. There are estimated to be more than a trillion comets in our solar system. Since they are lighter than asteroids, and have water-rich and carbon-rich compositions, many scientists have speculated that cometary impact may have brought water, the atmosphere, and even life to Earth.

The importance of monitoring near-Earth objects is highlighted by a number of recent events, where asteroids or comets nearly collided with Earth, or exploded in the planet's atmosphere. Several "Tunguska style" atmospheric explosions, where meteorites exploded in the atmosphere and formed air blasts have been noted, including the events in 1930 over the Amazon River, 1965 over southeastern Canada, in 1965 over Lake Huron, 1967 in Alberta, Canada, in Russia in 1992, Italy in 1993, Spain in 1994, Russia and the Mediterranean in 2002, and Washington in 2004. Other asteroid encounters were luckily near misses, where larger asteroids narrowly escaped collision with Earth. In 1972, an asteroid estimated to be 6–30 feet (2–10 m) in diameter entered Earth's atmosphere above Salt Lake City, Utah, formed a huge fireball that raced across the daytime sky, and exited the atmosphere near Calgary in Alberta, Canada. The geometry of the orbit was such that the meteorite just grazed the outer parts of the atmosphere, getting as close to the surface as 36 miles (58 km). In 1989, the 1,000 foot (300 m) diameter Apollo asteroid 4581 Asclepius crossed the exact place Earth had just passed through six hours earlier, missing the planet by a mere 400,000 miles (700,000 km). If an object that size collided with Earth, the results would have been catastrophic. On June 14, 2002, a 165–400 foot (50–120 m) diameter asteroid named 2002 MN passed unnoticed at a distance of 75,000 miles (120,700 km), one third the distance to the moon. Remarkably, this asteroid was not known until three days after it passed that closely to Earth. On July 3, 2006, another asteroid, named 2004 XP14, passed at about 248,000 miles (400,000 km), moving at a velocity of 10.5 miles per second (17 km/sec).

Several asteroids are known to be on near-collision courses with Earth. These include 99942 Apophis, which will pass within 20,000 miles (32,000 km) of Earth but will miss the planet. However, it may come closer in 2036, with a possible impact on that orbit. The chances of impact are estimated to be 1 in 43,000, making 99942 Apophis a Level O danger on the Torino impact hazard scale, shown in the table below. On March 16, 2880, asteroid 29075, with a diameter of 0.7–0.9 miles (1.1–1.4 km) will pass closely to Earth. Some models suggest that this asteroid has a 1 in 300 chance of hitting the planet, posing a significant

Torino Hazard Scale for Near Earth Objects	
SCALE	DESCRIPTION OF HAZARD
	NO HAZARD
0	The likelihood of a collision is zero, or is so low as to be effectively zero. Also applies to small objects such as meteors and bodies that burn up in the atmosphere as well as infrequent meteorite falls that rarely cause damage.
	NORMAL
1	A routine discovery in which a pass near Earth is predicted that poses no unusual level of danger. Current calculations show the chance of collision is extremely unlikely with no cause for public attention or public concern. New telescopic observations very likely will lead to reassignment to Level 0.
	MERITING ATTENTION BY ASTRONOMERS
2	A discovery, which may become routine with expanded searches, of an object making a somewhat close but not highly unusual pass near Earth. While meriting attention by astronomers, there is no cause for public attention or public concern as an actual collision is very unlikely. New telescopic observations very likely will lead to reassignment to Level 0.
3	A close encounter, meriting attention by astronomers. Current calculations give a 1 percent or greater chance of collision capable of localized destruction. Most likely, new telescopic observations will lead to reassignment to Level 0. Attention by public and by public officials is merited if the encounter is less than a decade away.
4	A close encounter, meriting attention by astronomers. Current calculations give a 1 percent or greater chance of collision capable of regional devastation. Most likely, new telescopic observations will lead to reassignment to Level 0. Attention by public and by public officials is merited if the encounter is less than a decade away.

SCALE	DESCRIPTION OF HAZARD
	THREATENING
5	A close encounter posing a serious, but still uncertain threat of regional devastation. Critical attention by astronomers is needed to determine conclusively whether a collision will occur. If the encounter is less than a decade away, governmental contingency planning may be warranted.
6	A close encounter by a large object posing a serious but still uncertain threat of a global catastrophe. Critical attention by astronomers is needed to determine conclusively whether a collision will occur. If the encounter is less than three decades away, governmental contingency planning may be warranted.
7	A very close encounter by a large object, which if occurring this century, poses an unprecedented but still uncertain threat of a global catastrophe. For such a threat in this century, international contingency planning is warranted, especially to determine urgently and conclusively whether a collision will occur.
	CERTAIN COLLISIONS
8	A collision is certain, capable of causing localized destruction for an impact over land or possibly a tsunami if close offshore. Such events occur on average between once per 50 years and once per several thousand years.
9	A collision is certain, capable of causing unprecedented regional devastation for a land impact or the threat of a major tsunami for an ocean impact. Such events occur on average between once per 10,000 years and once per 100,000 years.
10	A collision is certain, capable of causing global climatic catastrophe that may threaten the future of civilization as we know it, whether impacting land or ocean. Such events occur on average once per 100,000 years, or less often.

threat for a catastrophic collision, with major changes to climate and possibly triggering mass extinctions. This asteroid has the highest probability of any known large objects of hitting Earth.

Conclusion

The chances of experiencing a meteorite impact on Earth are small, but the risks associated with large impacts are extreme. Small objects hit Earth many times every day but burn up in the atmosphere. Events that release enough energy to destroy a city happen about once every thousand years, while major impacts that can significant alter Earth's climate happen every 300,000 years. Truly catastrophic impacts that cause mass extinctions, death of at least 25 percent of the world's population, and could lead to the end of the human race occur about every 100 million years.

Specific hazards from impacts include atmospheric shock waves and air blasts, major earthquakes, monstrous tsunamis, and global firestorms that throw so much soot in the air the impact is followed by a global winter that could last years. Carbon dioxide can be released by impacts as well, and then can act as greenhouse gases leading to global warming.

More than 20,000 near-Earth objects are thought to have a potential to collide with Earth, and more than 150 of these are larger than half a mile (1 km) across. A variety of programs to detect and track these near-Earth objects is under way, yet most meteorite impacts and near collisions in the past few years have been complete surprises. If a large asteroid is found to be on a collision course with Earth, several strategies have been devised that may be able to move the object out of its collision course with Earth. The asteroid could be attacked with nuclear weapons that could vaporize the object, removing the threat. However, this could also break up the asteroid and send thousands of smaller, now radioactive, fragments to Earth. If nuclear weapons are detonated near the asteroid, the force of the explosions may be enough to push it out of its collision course. A massive spacecraft could be crashed into the asteroid, changing its momentum and moving it from orbit. It might be possible to install rocket propulsion systems on the asteroid, and have it steer itself out of Earth orbit. A variety of other techniques have been proposed to deflect asteroids, including beaming solar radiation at the body, or attaching thermal blankets or sails, to have the solar radiation pressure move the asteroid out of its collision course.

Summary

Understanding the origin of Earth, the planets, Sun, and other bodies in the solar system is a fundamental yet complex problem that has intrigued scientists and philosophers for centuries. Most of the records from the earliest history of Earth have been lost to tectonic reworking and erosion, so most of what we know about the formation of Earth and solar system comes from the study of meteorites, Earth's Moon, and observations of the other planets and interstellar gas clouds.

The solar system displays many general trends with increasing distance from the Sun, and systematic changes like these imply that the planets were not captured gravitationally by the Sun, but rather formed from a single event that occurred about 4.6 billion years ago. The nebular theory for the origin of the solar system suggests that a large spinning cloud of dust and gas formed and began to collapse under its own gravitational attraction. As it collapsed, it began to spin faster to conserve angular momentum (much like ice skaters spin faster when they pull their arms in to their chest), and eventually formed a disk. Collisions between particles in the disk formed proto-planets and a protosun, which then had larger gravitational fields than surrounding particles, and began to sweep up and accrete loose particles.

The condensation theory states that particles of interstellar dust (many of which formed in older supernova) act as condensation nuclei that grow through accretion of other particles to form small planetsimals that then have a greater gravitational field that attracts and accretes other planetsimals and dust. Some collisions cause accretion, other collisions are hard and cause fragmentation and breaking up of the colliding bodies. The Jovian planets became so large that their gravitational fields were able to attract and accrete even free hydrogen and helium in the solar nebula.

The main differences between the planets with distance from the Sun are explained by this condensation theory, since the temperature of the solar nebula would have decreased away from the center where the Sun formed. The temperature determines which materials condense out of the nebula, so the composition of the planets was determined by the temperature at their position of formation in the nebula. The inner terrestrial planets are made of rocky and metallic material because high temperatures near the center of the nebula only allowed the rocky and metallic material to condense from the nebula. Farther out, water and ammonia ices also condensed out of the nebula, because temperatures were cooler at greater distances from the early Sun.

Early in the evolution of the solar system, the Sun was in a T-Tauri stage and possessed a strong solar wind that blew away most gases from the solar nebula, including the early atmospheres of the inner planets. Gravitational dynamics caused many of the early planetsimals to orbits in the Oort Cloud, where most comets and many meteorites are found. Some of these bodies have eccentric orbits that occasionally bring them into the inner solar system, and it is thought that collisions with comets and smaller molecules brought the present atmospheres and oceans to Earth and the other terrestrial planets. Thus air and water, some of the basic building blocks of life, were added to the planet after it formed, being thrown in from deep space of the Oort Cloud.

There are several different main types of meteorites. Stony meteorites include chondrites, which are very primitive and ancient meteorites made of silicate minerals like those common in Earth's crust and mantle, but chondrites contain small spherical objects known as chondrules. These chondrules contain frozen droplets of material that are thought to be remnants of the early solar nebula from which Earth and other planets initially condensed. Achondrites are similar to chondrites in mineralogy, except they do not contain the chondritic spheres. Iron meteorites are made of an iron-nickel alloy with textures that suggest they formed from slow crystallization inside a large asteroid or small planet that has since been broken into billions of small pieces, probably by an impact with another object. Stony-Irons are meteorites that contain mixtures of stony and iron components, and probably formed near the core-mantle boundary of the broken planet or asteroid. Almost all meteorites found on Earth are stony varieties.

The largest impact event of a meteorite or comet with Earth in roughly the past century occurred on June 30, 1908, when a huge explosion rocked a very remote area of central Siberia centered near the Tunguska River. After years of study and debate it is now thought that this huge explosion was produced by fragments of Comet Encke that broke off the main body, and exploded in the air about five miles (8 km) above the Siberian Plains. The Tunguska event began with a huge fireball moving westward across Siberia. Next, an explosion rocked the remote Tunguska region, with reports of the explosion and pressure waves being felt more than 600 miles (965 km) away. People who were hundreds of miles (km) from the site of the explosion were knocked down, and a huge 12-mile (20 km) high column of fire was visible for more than 400 miles (650 km). Seismometers recorded the impact, and barometers around the world recorded the air pressure wave as it traveled two times around the globe. The impact caused a strange, bright, unexplained glow to light the night skies in Scotland and Sweden. Several years after the impact, a scientific expedition to the remote region discovered that many trees were charred and knocked down in a 2,000 square mile (5,180 km^2) area, with near total destruction in the center 500 square miles (1,300 km^2). Many theories were advanced to explain the strange findings, and more than 50 years later in 1958 a new expedition to Tunguska found small melted globules of glass and metal, identified as pieces of an exploded meteorite or asteroid.

The geological record of impacts on the surface of Earth reveals more than 200 well-preserved impact structures, although many more have been eroded or buried beneath younger sediments. Most of these craters are relatively small, up to a couple of miles (several km) across, and consist of a simple crater with upturned or overturned rocks along the crater rim, where the force of the impact excavated the crater and threw the rocks from the inside to the edges. The most famous example of a small impact crater is Meteor Crater in Arizona. Larger craters can be tens or hundreds of miles (km) across, and have a more complex structure. Examples of complex impact structures include Manicougan in Canada, and Vredefort in South Africa. Both have multiple rings of faulted rocks surrounding the internal crater, which typically has an uplifted peak at its center.

The Chicxulub crater on Mexico's Yucatán Peninsula is a large complex crater that formed by an impact with Earth 66 million years ago.

This event generated an atmospheric blast, huge earthquakes, a monstrous tsunami, global firestorms followed by a global winter, then perhaps a global warming episode. The impact, with all its chaos, struck at a time that the planet's biosphere was stressed, and was more than many life-forms could handle. Many species went extinct, including the dinosaurs. Examination of the geological record of life on Earth reveals that there have been several mass extinction events, and that in most cases, it seems that if a large meteorite impact occurs at a time when the global environment is stressed, from climate change, massive volcanism, or other factors, that a mass extinction event may occur. In contrast, if a moderate-sized impact occurs when the biosphere is robust, there is less effect, as may be shown by the lack of a known extinction event associated with the Manicougan impact structure in Canada.

Small objects ranging from dust particles to asteroids a few tens of feet (few m) across enter Earth's atmosphere every day, usually burning up during their entry. There are roughly 20,000 significant near-Earth objects that could potentially strike the planet, and about 2,000 of these are larger than a half mile (1 km), potentially capable of causing a major planet-wide catastrophe. Efforts are being made to monitor near-Earth objects, to know if any are approaching Earth. The hazards of impact events are shown by many examples, with the general hazards being associated with large air blasts from bolides that explode in the atmosphere, and powerful earthquakes, tsunamis, global firestorms, and ejection of huge amounts of dust and soot into the atmosphere causing global winters. Collision of a body a mile (1.6 km) in diameter with Earth has the potential to kill at least a quarter (1.6 billion) of the human race, with larger events being even more catastrophic. Events of this size happen about once every three million years, and the larger impacts that cause mass extinctions about once every one hundred million years. Techniques to deflect asteroids on an Earth-impact course are being studied by NASA, the United States Air Force, and the European Space Agency. The techniques include ideas to blast apart the asteroids with direct targeting using nuclear weapons, to deflect the asteroid with blasts to one side of the object, and to crash massive spacecraft into the asteroid to change its momentum and collision course. Other ideas include mounting rockets on the asteroid to steer it away, adding reflective blankets or sails on parts of the body to create a radiation pressure that could move the object, and to direct solar energy at the asteroid to vaporize its surface and change its orbit. None of these have been tested, but vigilance for the future protection of the planet from impact hazards would suggest that such systems should be in place in the event of an asteroid emergency. In the past few years, several very large asteroids approached very close to Earth, and were not detected until they were hours or days away, or even after they passed. Therefore, having asteroid deflection programs in place, ready to call up in a moment's notice, is a preferable mitigation strategy over waiting until an asteroid is bearing down on a densely inhabited metropolis on Earth.

Appendix

The Geologic Timescale

Era	Period	Epoch	Age (millions of years)	First Life-forms	Geology
		Holocene	0.01		
	Quaternary				
Cenozoic		Pleistocene	3	Humans	Ice age
		Pliocene	11	Mastodons	Cascades
		Neogene			
		Miocene	26	Saber-toothed tigers	Alps
	Tertiary	Oligocene	37		
		Paleogene			
		Eocene	54	Whales	
		Paleocene	65	Horses, Alligators	Rockies
	Cretaceous		135		
Mesozoic	Jurassic		210	Birds	Sierra Nevada
				Mammals	Atlantic
				Dinosaurs	
	Triassic		250		
	Permian		280	Reptiles	Appalachians
	Pennsylvanian		310		Ice age
				Trees	
	Carboniferous				
Paleozoic	Mississippian		345	Amphibians	Pangaea
				Insects	
	Devonian		400	Sharks	
	Silurian		435	Land plants	Laurasia
	Ordovician		500	Fish	
	Cambrian		544	Sea plants	Gondwana
				Shelled animals	
			700	Invertebrates	Rodinia
Proterozoic			2500	Metazoans	
			3500	Earliest life	
Archean			4000		Oldest rocks
			4600		Meteorites

Glossary

accretion—The gravitational accumulation of dust, gas, and rocky bodies such as asteroids to a larger body such as a planet.

achondrite—A stony meteorite that does not contain chondrules.

Amors—Asteroids that orbit between Earth and Mars, but do not cross Earth's orbit.

aphelion—The point in an orbit that is furthest from the Sun.

Apollo asteroids—Asteroids that orbit less than one astronomical unit with periods longer than one year.

Archea—Simple organisms that appeared on Earth by 3.85 billion years ago.

Archean—The first eon of geological time, stretching from the end of the Hadean until the start of the Proterozoic eon at 2.5 billion years ago.

asteroid—A rocky or metallic body in space orbiting the Sun.

astronomical unit (AU)—The distance from the Sun to Earth, or 93 million miles (150 million km).

Aten asteroids—Asteroids that orbit at less than one astronomical unit and have an orbital period of less than one year, and some of these cross Earth's orbit.

big bang theory—Theory for the origin of the universe, where the universe originated 10–20 billion years ago in a single explosive event in which the entire universe suddenly exploded out of nothing, reaching a pea-sized supercondensed state with a temperature of 10 billion million million degrees Celsius in (10^{-36}) of a second after the big bang.

bolide—A name for any unidentified object entering the planet's atmosphere.

brachiopod—Two-shelled marine invertebrate organisms.

breccia—A fragmented rock produced by the breaking of pre-existing rocks.

bryozoans—Colonial organisms with hard skeletons of calcium carbonate, resembling coral.

calcium-aluminum inclusions—A group of very high-temperature minerals found inside some chondrules, typically exhibiting textures like concentric skins of an onion.

carbonaceous chondrites—Chondritic meteorites that contain organic material such as hydrocarbons in rings and chains, and amino acids.

Centaurs—A group of asteroids with orbits that have highly eccentric orbits that extend beyond yet cross the orbits of Jupiter and Saturn, thus can potentially collide with these planets.

chondrite—A stony meteorite containing chondrules.

chondrules—Small lumps in chondritic meteorites, that are thought to represent melt droplets that formed before the meteorite fragments were accreted to asteroids, and thus represent some of the oldest material in the solar system.

coma—The gaseous rim of a comet, from which the tail extends.

comet—An icy or mixed icy and rocky body that orbits the Sun, and typically emits a long tail on its close approach to the Sun.

conodonts—Extinct chordate, toothlike fossils that were part of a larger organism of the Class Conodonta.

cosmic background radiation—Faint electromagnetic radiation that fills the universe, discovered in 1965, radiating as a thermal black body at 2.75 degrees Kelvin. It is thought to be a remnant of the big bang.

dark matter—A hypothetical form of matter of unknown composition but probably consisting of elemental particles, and that does not emit or reflect electromagnetic radiation, so can only be detected by observing its gravitational effects.

dwarf planet—A celestial body that (a) is in orbit around the Sun, (b) has sufficient mass for its self-gravity to overcome rigid body forces so that it assumes a hydrostatic equilibrium (nearly round) shape, (c) has not cleared the neighborhood around its orbit, and (d) is not a satellite.

ecliptic plane—The relatively flat plane that most of the planets orbits around the Sun are contained within.

ejecta—Material thrown out of an impact crater during an impact event.

eukaryotes—Simple single cell organisms containing a cell nucleus and membrane bound organelles.

fireball—Streak of light that moves across sky, produced by a meteorite or comet burning up in atmosphere.

Gondwana—A supercontinent, where most of the planet's continental mass was grouped together at the end of the Proterozoic and beginning of the Phanerozoic.

Hadean Era—The earliest time in Earth history, ranging from accretion at 4.56 billion years ago, until the time of the oldest rocks preserved at 3.96 billion years ago.

hot spot—An area of unusually active magmatic activity that is not associated with a plate boundary. Hot spots are thought to form above a plume of magma rising from deep in the mantle.

hydrosphere—The sphere containing all the water on Earth.

impact crater—A generally bowl-shaped depression excavated by the impact of a meteorite or comet with Earth.

impact glass—A glass produced by the sudden melting and homogenization and sudden cooling of rock during a meteorite impact event.

impactor—A general name for an object that strikes and creates a crater in another object.

inflationary theory—A modification of the big bang theory, and suggests that the universe underwent a period of rapid expansion immediately after the big bang.

iron meteorites—Composed mostly of metallic material, and mixtures called stony-iron meteorites.

Kuiper Belt—A distant part of the solar system extending from 30–49 astronomical units, and containing many comets and asteroids.

mass extinction—The death of flora and flora species and individuals on a global scale.

megaton—A mass equal to 1,000,000 tons, at 2,000 pounds per ton in the United States. One ton is equal to 0.907 metric tonnes.

meteor—Streak of light in the sky formed by the burning of a meteorite or comet as it moves through Earth's atmosphere.

meteorite—Rocky or metallic body that has fallen to Earth from space.

mid-ocean ridge system—A 40,000-mile (65,000-km) long mountain ridge that runs through all the major oceans on the planet. The mid-ocean ridge system includes vast outpourings of young lava on the ocean floor, and represents places where new oceanic crust is being generated by plate tectonics.

nucleus—As used here, the inner part of a comet, consisting of rock and ices.

Oort Cloud—A roughly spherical region containing many comets and other objects, extending from about 60 AU to beyond 50,000 AU, or about 1,000 times the distance from the Sun to Pluto, or about a light-year.

ostracods—Shrimplike fossils of the class Crustacea.

perihelion—The point in an orbit closest to the Sun.

photosynthesis—Process by which plants and some bacteria use sunlight to produce sugar.

planet—A celestial body that (a) is in orbit around the Sun, (b) has sufficient mass for its self-gravity to overcome rigid body forces so that it assumes a hydrostatic equilibrium (nearly round) shape, and (c) has cleared the neighborhood around its orbit.

planetsimal—A proto-planet growing in the solar nebula.

Prokaryotic bacteria—Single celled organisms lacking a cell nucleus.

Proterozoic—The second eon of geological time, stretching from the end of the Archean eon at 2.5 billion years ago until the start of the Paleozoic at 540 million years ago.

proto-planet—A large body in the solar nebula that is in the process of growing by accretion into a planet.

pseudotachylites—Glassy melt rocks that form along faults and from impact craters.

resonances—Stable orbits where asteroids can remain for long periods of time, produced by an effect of the gravity and different orbital periods of the larger planets in the inner solar system.

seafloor spreading—The process of producing new oceanic crust, as volcanic basalt pours out of the depths of Earth, filling the gaps generated by diverging plates. Beneath the mid-oceanic ridges, magma rises from depth in the mantle and forms chambers filled with magma just below the crest of the ridges. The magma in these chambers erupts out through cracks in the roof of the chambers, and forms extensive lava flows on the surface. As the two different plates on either side of the magma chamber move apart, these lava flows continuously fill in the gap between the diverging plates, creating new oceanic crust.

shatter cone—A group of fractures in a rock that forms a cone shape, and points toward the source of an explosion, such as a meteorite impact.

SNC meteorites—A class of meteorites that includes shergottites, nakhlites, and chassignites, and are believed to have originated from Mars and the Moon, being ejected by impact events on those planets, and landing on Earth.

solar nebula—In the early history of the solar system, the glowing cloud of dust, gas, and growing planets that formed during collapse of a gas cloud, with the protosun at the center and the planets orbiting around the Sun.

spaceguard—A term that refers to a number of different efforts to search for and monitor near-Earth objects.

standard model—Model for the origin of the universe, stating that it formed 14 billion years ago in the big bang. Galaxies and stars form 4.8 percent of the universe, 22.7 percent of the universe consists of dark matter, and 72.5 percent of the universe is nonmatter.

stony meteorites—Meteorites made of material typical of igneous rocks, such as minerals of olivine and pyroxene.

tsunami—Giant long-wavelength wave, can be produced by the impact of a meteorite with the ocean, or by other means such as earthquakes.

T-Tauri stage—A stage of stellar evolution where a very young (< 10 million years old) small star, less than 3 solar masses, is still undergoing gravitational contraction. This is an intermediate stage in stellar evolution between a protostar and a main sequence star, which the Sun is presently.

Widmannstatten texture—A crisscross texture best shown polished metallic surfaces of iron meteorites, produced by intergrown blades of iron and nickel minerals, with the size of the blades is related to the cooling rate of the minerals.

Further Reading

BOOKS

Albritton, C. C. Jr. *Catastrophic Episodes in Earth History.* London: Chapman and Hale. 1989. A book that discusses the different mass extinction events and their causes.

Alvarez, Walter. *T Rex and the Crater of Doom.* Princeton, N.J.: Princeton University Press, 1997. A novel-like book that discusses the discovery and understanding that a meteorite impact may have led to the Cretaceous-Tertiary extinction.

Angelo, Joseph A. *Encyclopedia of Space and Astronomy.* New York: Facts On File, 2006. This is a comprehensive, high school to college level encyclopedia covering thousands of topics in Astronomy.

Chaisson, Eric, and Steve McMillan. *Astronomy Today,* 2nd ed. Upper Saddle River, N.J.: Prentice Hall College Div., 1996. A college level textbook on astronomy.

Cox, Donald, and James Chestek. *Doomsday Asteroid: Can We Survive?* New York: Prometheus Books, 1996. A good treatment of the possibility of Earth being hit by an asteroid, and the chances of surviving.

Dressler, B. O., R. A. F. Grieve, and V. L. Sharpton, eds. *Large Meteorite Impacts and Planetary Evolution.* Boulder, Colo.: Geological Society of America Special Paper 293, 1994. This is a collection of technical papers on the effects of large impacts on the evolution of planetary crusts.

Eldredge, N. *Fossils: The Evolution and Extinction of Species.* Princeton, N.J.: Princeton University Press, 1997. A comprehensive text on the evolution, and causes of mass extinctions.

Elkins-Tanton, Linda T. *Asteroids, Meteorites, and Comets.* New York: Facts On File, 2006. This is a good high school book that covers the characteristics, formation, and evolution of asteroids, meteorites, and comets.

Gehrels, T., ed. *Hazards Due to Comets and Asteroids.* Tucson, Ariz.: University of Arizona Press, 1994. A collection of technical papers on the different hazards of impacts on Earth, including atmospheric effects, tsunami, mass extinctions, and others.

Hodge, Paul. *Meteorite Craters and Impact Structures of the Earth.* Cambridge, U.K.: Cambridge University Press, 1994. This is a well-illustrated book that catalogs and describes known impact structures on Earth.

Krinov, E. L. *Giant Meteorites.* Oxford: Pergamon Press, 1966. This book describes some of the meteorite impacts known in the 1960s, and includes some eyewitness accounts of the Tunguska impact event.

Kusky, T. M. *Encyclopedia of Earth Science.* New York: Facts On File, 2004. A comprehensive encyclopedia of Earth sciences written for college and high school audiences, and the general public.

Mark, Kathleen. *Meteorite Craters.* Tucson, Ariz.: University of Arizona Press, 1987. A catalog and historical account of the recognition of meteorite craters.

Melosh, H. J. *Impact Cratering: A Geologic Process.* New York: Oxford University Press, 1988. This book describes many of the physical principles associated with the formation of large and small impact craters.

Morrison, David, Clark Chapman, and Paul Slovic. "The Impact Hazard." In *Hazards Due to Comets and Asteroids,* edited by T. Gehrels, 59–91. Tucson, Ariz.: University of Arizona Press, 1994. This article deals with the probabilities of impacts of different sizes hitting Earth.

Project Icarus. *An MIT Student Project in Systems Engineering.* Cambridge, Mass.: The MIT Press, 1968. This book describes one of the first asteroid deflection systems, devised by students at MIT.

Spencer, John R., and Jacqueline Mitton. *The Great Comet Crash: The Impact of Comet Shoemaker-Levy 9 on Jupiter.* Cambridge, U.K.: Cambridge University Press, 1995. This is a detailed book documenting the impact of a comet on Jupiter.

Stanley, Steven M. *Earth and Life through Time.* New York: W. H. Freeman, 1986. This book describes the different life-forms extant on Earth in different geological periods, and the extinction events that separate different stages.

Thomas, Paul J., Christopher F. Chyba, and Christopher P. McKay, eds. *Comets and the Origin and Evolution of Life.* New York: Springer-Verlag. 1997. A collection of technical papers on the possibility that life came to Earth on comets.

Wasson, John T. *Meteorites: Their Record of Early Solar-System History.* New York: W. H. Freeman, 1985. This is a technical book covering the chemistry of meteorites and the physics of their orbits and falls to Earth.

JOURNAL ARTICLES

Bottke, W. F., D. Vokrouhlicky, D. Nesvorny. "An asteroid breakup 160 Myr ago as the probably source of the K-T impactor." *Nature* 449 (2007):

23–25. This paper describes evidence that the meteorite that hit the Yucatán at Chicxulub, causing the K-T mass extinction, was a piece of a larger asteroid that broke up in a collision 160 million years ago.

Chapman, C. R., and D. Morrison. "Impacts on the Earth by asteroids and comets: Assessing the hazard." *Nature* 367 (1994): 33–39. This article describes the risk of global catastrophe by giant and smaller impacts of meteorites on Earth.

Erwin, D. H.. "The Permo-Traissic extinction." *Nature* 367 (1994): 231–236. A description of the species that went extinct at the most significant mass extinction of all time, and possible causes.

Hildebrand, Alan R., Glen T. Penfield, David A. Kring, Mark Pilkington, Antonio C. Zanoguera, Stein B. Jacobsen, and William V. Boynton. "Chicxulub Crater; a possible Cretaceous-Tertiary boundary impact crater on the Yucatan Peninsula, Mexico." *Geology* 19 (1991): 867–871. This paper describes the discovery and geology of the Chicxulub Crater.

Pope, K. O., A. C. Ocampo, G. L. Kinsland, and R. Smith. "Surface expression of the Chicxulub crater." *Geology* 24 (1996): 527–530. This paper describes some of the subtle topographic features including sinkholes that are associated with the Chicxulub crater.

WEB SITES

In the past few years numerous Web sites with information about meteorite impacts, asteroids, and comets have appeared. Most of these Web sites are free, and include historical information about their orbits, observations, tracking, and disasters from meteorite impacts around the world, and educational material. The sites listed below have interesting information, statistics, and graphics about these hazards. This book may serve as a useful companion while surfing through the information on the Internet when encountering unfamiliar phrases, terms, or concepts that are not fully explained on the Web site. The following list of Web sites is recommended to help enrich the content of this book and make your exploration of asteroids, comets, and meteorite impact more enjoyable. From these Web sites you will also be able to link to a large variety of impact- and space-related sites. Every effort has been made to ensure the accuracy of the information provided for these Web sites. However, due to the dynamic nature of the Internet, changes might occur, and any inconvenience is regretted.

Geological Survey of Canada, Earth Impact Database. The Geological Survey of Canada has compiled an Earth Impact database. The database is regularly maintained, and contains maps and images of various impact craters. Available online. URL: http://www.unb.ca/passc/ ImpactDatabase. Accessed on February 17, 2008.

Lunar and Planetary Laboratory, University of Arizona. Web site has an extensive list of information about meteors, meteorites, impacts, and links to other sites. Site is run by the Students for the Exploration and Development of Space (SEDS). Available online. URL: http://seds.lpl. arizona.edu/nineplanets/nineplanets/meteorites.html. Accessed on February 17, 2008.

National Aeronautic and Space Administration (NASA). NASA's Web site on Lunar and Planetary Science. This Web site is a great place to start exploring the solar system, with links to information about all the planets, major asteroids, near-Earth asteroid tracking systems, and current and past missions to asteroids. Available online. URL: http:// nssdc.gsfc.nasa.gov/planetary/planets/asteroidpage.html. Accessed on February 17, 2008.

National Aeronautic and Space Administration (NASA). NASA's Web site on Natural Hazards. Earth scientists around the world use NASA satellite imagery to better understand the causes and effects of natural hazards including risks of asteroid, comet, and meteorite impact. This site posts many public domain images to help people visualize where and when natural hazards occur, and to help mitigate their effects. All images in this section are freely available to the public for reuse or re-publication. Available online. URL: http://earthobservatory.nasa.gov/ NaturalHazards/. Accessed on January 30, 2008.

National Aeronautic and Space Administration (NASA), Near-Earth Object Program. In 1998 NASA initiated a program called the Near-Earth Object Program, whose aim is to catalog potentially hazardous asteroids that could present a hazard to Earth. This program uses five large telescopes to search the skies for asteroids that pose a threat to Earth, and to calculate their mass and orbits. Available online. URL: http://neo.jpl.nasa.gov. Accessed February 17, 2008.

National Oceanographic and Atmospheric Administration, Hazards Research. Web site about satellite and information services, including data on space weather, solar events, and observations of Earth from space. Available online. URL: http://ngdc.noaa.gov/ngdc.html. Accessed on February 17, 2008.

Natural Hazards Observer. This Web site is the online version of the periodical, *The Natural Hazards Observer,* the bimonthly periodical of the Natural Hazards Center. It covers current disaster issues; new international, national, and local disaster management, mitigation, and education programs; hazards research; political and policy developments; new information sources and Web sites; upcoming conferences; and recent publications. Distributed to more than 15,000 subscribers in the United States and abroad via printed copies, their Web site focuses on news regarding human adaptation and response to natural hazards and other catastrophic events and provides a forum for concerned individuals to express opinions and generate new ideas through invited personal articles. Available online: URL: http://www.colorado.edu/hazards/o/. Accessed on February 17, 2008.

Index

Note: Page numbers in *italic* indicate illustrations, *m* indicates a map and *t* indicates a table.